Something Wonderful

IS ABOUT TO HAPPEN . . .

True stories of people who found
happiness in unexpected places

Robin L. Silverman

To Becky & Denny —
Wishing you a
wonder-full life!
= ♡ =

Robin L.
Silverman

Adams Media Corporation
Avon, Massachusetts

To my daughters, Amanda and Erica.
Thank you for the wonders you are.

Published by
Adams Media Corporation
57 Littlefield Street, Avon, MA 02322 U.S.A.
www.adamsmedia.com

ISBN: 1-58062-620-3

Printed in Canada.

J I H G F E D C B

Library of Congress Cataloging-in-Publication Data
Silverman, Robin Landew.
Something wonderful is about to happen / by Robin L. Silverman.
p.   cm.
ISBN 1-58062-620-3
1. Women—Conduct of life. I. Title.
BJ1610   .S485 2003
158—dc21 2002011337

This book is available at quantity discounts for bulk purchases.
For information, call 1-800-872-5627.

Contents

≈

Contents

Introduction

~

We live in rapidly changing times. What was true yesterday is no longer true today. Things we once knew for certain are now shadows. When we try to grab them with our hands, our heads, or our hearts, we hold nothing but ghosts of memory.

The same can be said of the future. We have no way of knowing for sure in what form it will arrive or if we will feel ready when it comes. Plans and goals are easily upset by what is on the evening news or in our medical files.

This is why the only reliable moment is now. But there is comfort here. Right here, we can see where we are. Right now, we know what we think and feel. Right away, we can direct what we are saying and doing, opening our senses and selves to wonder if we want to do so.

In many ways, we have no choice. Worry makes us sick and tired, for there is no way to constantly battle invisible demons without mental, emotional, and spiritual fatigue. Keeping up our guard is limiting, exhausting. Nor can we spend too much time or effort looking back without feeling the need to run away faster from regret and anger. We can try to forget what we should have done or said, but the echoes of grudges and insufficiencies seem to find us wherever we go.

Yes, it is time for our suffering to stop and for something wonderful to happen. Today. This minute. And I can tell you with confidence that it's possible, because I've had it happen to me and have seen it happen to dozens of other people. Something wonderful happens when we stop running from what we want, when we listen to life's whispered yearnings for us and choose to respond. It comes when we forget who we think we are supposed to be and act on the amazing stuff we are made of. It happens when we stop wrestling with life and start to embrace it instead.

Ironically, many people believe that wonderful things come from outside ourselves, as if they are dropped from the sky like cosmic Halloween candy. That belief leaves us restless and unhappy, since it makes it far too easy to make wonder seem like a stroke of luck or a whim of God. We're no better off if we think that wonderful experiences are gifts to us from other people, since our tendency is to regard anything we receive from others as either wrong or lacking in some way. Wonders don't start when someone says, "Here you go." They begin the moment we stand up straight, open our souls, and announce, "Here I am."

Wonder does not happen to us; it happens through us in one of two ways. The first is when we become heroes to ourselves, rising above one of life's many challenges. When we do the thing we think we cannot do or shift our experience by raising our perspective, wonder is born. The second way to experience wonder is more subtle and, for many people, more elusive. Wonder arrives when we simply allow it to enter our lives, when we turn off our resistance and negativity just long enough to welcome and acknowledge its presence. This usually happens when we are at our most broken, tired, or exposed, when we are too weak to battle life. Since most of us keep up our guard much of the time, wonder only occasionally happens this way. Only one thing is certain: When we are open to it, either through innocence, desire, or vulnerability, or when we rise up to grab it, wonder arrives without hesitation or qualification.

Now that we know how wonder arrives, the next question is obvious: When? The answer is equally simple: whenever we're ready. The problem, however, is that simply making the decision is not enough. If you've never experienced wonder, you may be frightened of something you've never consciously known. If you like to be in control, you may resist the idea of allowing an event that you neither plan nor direct to enter your life. If you have spent your years wrestling with life, you may harbor serious doubts about whether something as pleasant as wonder is even possible. Fear not. The fact that you've picked up this book is proof enough that even if you're not quite ready, you're curious. And in time, you may be willing to let a little wonder into your life.

Regardless of the state of your life or your state of mind right now, wonder is already here. Turn the page, and you'll see for yourself. It happens a lot. It could happen to you.

So read a story or two. Try one of the Love Lights, exercises that are designed to help you welcome something wonderful into your own life. You'll soon see that wonder is staring you right in the face. It is in this place, this moment. What you'll see is that it is common for people to find what they are looking for right where they are. Dorothy did not have to get any special power from the Wizard of Oz in order to go home. Neither do you.

Today is the best day of your life to travel "home" to yourself. All that you need to be happy, healthy, fulfilled — wonderful — is within you right now. Your adventure has started. So make a wish, including the one you never dared say aloud. Decide to see yourself or your situation differently. Take the first step toward whatever you think you cannot do.

Something Wonderful Is About to Happen . . .

Your banged-up, bruised life could probably use a few more wonderful happenings. So could our planet. I am looking forward to hearing what these inspiring stories and ideas can do for you and will do my best to respond if you write to me:

Robin L. Silverman
P.O. Box 13135
Grand Forks, ND 58208-3135

I wish you all things wonderful,
Robin L. Silverman

Finding Clancy

The wonder of a lifelong wish come true

When we are young, we don't always get what we want.
That's because we want everything, all the time, and actually believe that it's possible both to have and enjoy it. We expect our parents to deliver every one of our hearts' desires, and they do so when they promise us that what we want will be ours "someday." Cleverly, they never specify when that day will be. So the days and nights roll on. Sometimes, our wishes are granted very quickly. Other times, they are not. Even when they are not made manifest for decades, the best wishes never die, but burn brightly in our hearts.

As adults, we often forget about the wishes we made when we were children. And we don't bother to make more because we are too busy trying to be "realistic." That's a shame, because wishes are what create hope, and without hope, the world is a stagnant, frustrating place. Grownups need to make wishes often so we can stay in touch with both our heads and our hearts. For when we do, we become like children again, growing and glowing.

If you know the value of making wishes, you can make wonderful things happen.

SANDI ALWAYS WANTED A DOG. As a young teen, she said, "When I grow up, I'm going to have a shaggy dog, and I am going to name him Clancy."

Years passed, and Sandi forgot about Clancy. She married and started her own home. Decades later, her husband brought a cat named Thomas into her life, and she treasured him.

Thomas would curl up contentedly in Sandi's art studio while she worked and purred with the comfort of her gentle hands stroking his silky coat.

More years passed. Thomas started to have health problems, and so did Sandi. One day, not long after Sandi had surgery for breast cancer, her cousin Debbie surprised her with a phone call. "I've been thinking a lot about you lately," Debbie said, "and I think you need a dog." Then she went on to describe the breed she thought Sandi should have: a Tibetan terrier. Debbie owned one and loved it and thought Sandi would feel similarly since the breed was created by Tibetan monks 2,000 years ago as "holy dogs." A Tibetan terrier in the household was supposed to bring good luck.

Debbie sent Sandi a picture of her dog, which looked a lot like the shaggy dog Sandi wished for as a child. Sandi kept the photo posted on the refrigerator for more than six months. Still, Sandi didn't think it was time for her to search for her dog because she and her husband, John, still had Thomas, who was requiring more and more of their energies. Eventually, she took down the picture. Once again, the idea of finding Clancy retreated to the back of her mind.

When Thomas died, Sandi soon longed for another pet. She found herself surfing everywhere on the Internet, looking at the Web sites of local animal shelters. She found no Tibetan terriers nearby; but before long, she knew the names and faces of practically every available dog in her area. Her yearning heart reached out to each and every one, and she grew increasingly distressed and tearful when a red line would appear through the photo of one of the dogs with the caption "humanely destroyed." Even though some of the dogs were shaggy, none looked like the pet she had imagined in her childhood.

Sandi agreed that a Tibetan terrier was probably the dog for her, so she kept searching more and more each day. But as she did, her desire to bring a dog into her life grew greater, and she became open to adopting something other than a Tibetan terrier. Still, none of the furry faces she saw sang to her effervescent spirit. "You know when you find the right dog," she says. "You just get a feeling in your heart."

Finally, Sandi knew the time was right for her to adopt. So she offered up a simple prayer: "God, please bring me the dog that is meant to be ours. I leave it in Your hands." She slept peacefully that night.

The next morning, something wonderful happened. Sandi began to search the Internet again and stumbled upon a Web site with a strange-sounding name: "Avenging Emma." It had links to many animal shelters. The final name at the bottom of the list was for a shelter in Nebraska called Hearts United for Animals. Although Sandi lived in Massachusetts, she was intrigued because the shelter said it would ship an animal "under the right circumstances."

Sandi started slowly paging through the Web site. On the sixth page, front and center, was a photo of an absolutely adorable black-and-white shaggy dog, a Tibetan terrier. The instant Sandi saw him, her heart started pounding. "All I kept feeling was, 'I'm your mama!' " she said. Then she scrolled down the photo. There, just beneath the shaggy face she instantly loved, was the dog's name.

Clancy.

Sandi quickly e-mailed the shelter to ask if Clancy was available for adoption, filled out their four-page adoption application, and faxed it to them. A few e-mail exchanges later, the shelter asked for a home inspection before they would approve the adoption. Sandi was happy to oblige and wanted it scheduled as soon as possible.

The shelter could find only one volunteer in the area to do the inspection. Within the week, she visited Sandi's home. As the two women were talking, another wonderful thing happened.

The volunteer said, "I have *never* felt this good about a matchup between a dog and owners." And then she asked how Sandi had heard of Hearts United for Animals.

Sandi told the volunteer about the prayer she had said and how the next day she was led to this "funny-sounding" Web site that linked her to the Hearts United for Animals homepage. The volunteer became very quiet for a moment. "By any chance, was that 'funny-sounding' Web site called 'Avenging Emma?' "

"Yes," Sandi said, surprised. "It was. Why?"

The volunteer smiled. "Because that's *my* Web site."

The circle was complete. The volunteer had led Sandi to Clancy, and now it was she who gave the final approval for the adoption. Within days, the people from the shelter drove Clancy three hours to the Kansas City airport so he could be on a nonstop flight to Boston. And today, Sandi, John, and Clancy are living happily ever after.

♡ *Love Light: Attracting New Friends*

When you want to bring someone or something new into your life, it is good to do what Sandi did. Clearly identify your hopes—in her case, having a shaggy dog named Clancy. Allow the feeling of having your wish come true to penetrate your heart. Get comfortable with the embodiment of your wish, for when you bring new friends into your life, they are likely to stay for a long, long time.

The next part is a little tricky. You must take your attention off the fact that they have *not* arrived in the form you want . . . yet. This is difficult for many people. In Sandi's case, she was searching for a Tibetan terrier. But as she browsed the pages of available dogs, she only noticed the lack of what she wanted—in other words, how many dogs *weren't* the breed or didn't have the look or feeling for which she hoped. The same is true with, say, relationships. There may be countless men or women around, but when you're waiting for love, all you can notice is who is not a likely candidate, not who is. When Sandi let go of her insistence on having a Tibetan terrier, telling God she simply wanted to love any dog that needed her, she opened the gate for wonder to enter. Suddenly, every dog became a possibility, and she received each one in her heart, if only for a few seconds. The possibility of having a new dog to love became a probability, which started to feel like an actuality. Sandi was totally comfortable and ready for her desire to be met. That's when life rushed in with its wholehearted "Yes!" including the breed her heart had truly desired.

So make your wish. Get comfortable with it. Let go of your resistance. And get ready. Something wonderful is going to happen.

Pennies from Heaven

The wonder of giving a little and getting a lot

$\mathcal{M}$ ost people are willing givers. We rarely think of giving money as easy or effortless, though, no matter what our net worth. That's because we often feel that no matter how much we give, we are expected to give more. The need is never satisfied. Enough is never enough.

I've never met a person who didn't want to be thought of as generous. But there are always bills to pay and uncertainties for which to save. It's not easy to relax and simply have fun with money without ever considering the consequences of spending it. We want to use our money to make others feel good, but how can we do that without making ourselves feel bad?

One way is to start with one cent. Just a penny. Offer it with love, and the feeling it buys multiplies a thousandfold.

ONE HUMID JULY MORNING, my twelve-year-old daughter, Erica, and I decided to take a walk in downtown Edgartown, Massachusetts, after breakfast.

"To shop?" she asked.

"No," I answered. "To make magic."

I reached into my purse and took out the six shiniest pennies I had and put three of them in her eager hand.

"Let's make someone feel wonderful," I said.

She looked at the coins. "How will three pennies make someone feel good?"

"When people find a penny on a sidewalk, they think they are lucky," I answered. "That makes them feel like a winner, as if they're about to be rewarded for all their hard work or good intentions. You know the rhyme: 'Find a penny, pick it up, and all the day you'll have good luck.' They get excited, and that makes them feel happy."

She was silent, thinking as we walked a little farther. I noticed that she had stopped looking in store windows and was now staring at the treasure in her hand. "Usually, you'll see people smile as they pick up a penny and put it in their pocket," I continued. "At that moment, they expect the best. And you know what? Something wonderful almost always happens to them."

Erica looked at me. "Why?"

"Because they start looking for it. A penny feels like a promise from life that says, 'There's something wonderful waiting for you. Get ready.' So the finder starts noticing more good things, and the bad things don't bother them as much. When they do that, they automatically feel better, and that makes the whole day feel 'luckier' to them."

"But how do we know who needs the pennies most?" Erica asked.

"We don't. One of the things about penny giving is that if you put it in someone's hand, they don't feel as lucky. It's the chance encounter with it that makes it wonderful. Let's just let them fall. The right person will find each one. Promise."

Erica walked along the sidewalk deliberately, as if trying to find the perfect crack or crevice to harbor her prize.

"Do I put it down or throw it?" she asked.

"You decide," I said. "I like to just drop mine and let them land where they may."

She fell back a few steps. I slowed my gait to wait for her while looking ahead for a spot to drop my first penny. Within seconds, I heard a cheerful *ping!* as Erica released her treasure.

"I did it! I did it!" she called as she came running up to me. She was as gleeful as she was at age five, when she first rode her two-wheel bike without falling.

We continued our walk with silent grins on our faces, secret partners in happiness. Suddenly, her smile faded.

"But what if no one finds it?" she asked.

"Oh, someone always does," I said. "To prove it, let's finish dropping all of them. Then we'll retrace our steps. I bet all of them will be gone."

The next five pennies fell like first rain, one shiny drop at a time. I released one by the corner drugstore. Erica let go of one of hers in front of the ice cream store. I walked over to the town square and opened my hand by the green park bench. Erica let her last penny roll off the stoop of the T-shirt shop. And I tossed my last one over my left shoulder to land silently into some soft, new grass.

No one ran up to us shouting, "Hey! You dropped some money!" No one around us even seemed to hear the soft chimes of the pennies as they touched ground. But somewhere deep within, we knew we were granting someone's wish. It was like tossing coins in a fountain, except that this time the hope was for another's happiness, not our own.

We stayed downtown for another hour, searching faces for signs of delight. A twelve-year-old boy stuffing a piece of gooey chocolate fudge into his mouth as he mounted his black dirt bike . . . the silver-haired woman in the nautical sweater carrying a tidy bag from the card shop . . . the smiling father with his two-year-old daughter perched on his shoulders . . . were they the lucky ones?

Then something wonderful happened. We retraced our steps and discovered that every one of the six pennies was gone, swept up, no doubt, by eager hearts and hands. Six strangers now felt lucky. Six people we would likely never meet had a penny in their pockets and the feeling that life was about to respond to them in some generous way. Six souls like ours were temporarily satisfied, secure that in some small way, everything would be all right.

When we got back to the house, Amanda, my older daughter, asked us what we had been up to. "We ate breakfast and dropped pennies," Erica said.

"Oh, that's so much fun!" Amanda gushed. "Did you see who got them?"

Erica shook her head and looked at me. I turned to Amanda. "We played the wonder game with them. You know, 'I wonder if that's the person who got the penny?' It's more fun to think that everyone could have found one rather than just a few people, even though we only made eight people happy today."

"You mean six, don't you?" Erica asked.

"No, eight," I said gently. "The six people who found our pennies—and you and me for all the fun we had dropping them. Feels good to give, doesn't it?"

She smiled. "Yep."

❧ *Love Light: Give Away*

If you like the feeling of giving away money but struggle with the worry that you may not have enough or be giving enough, try this:

First, start paying attention to how much money you waste. We all do this with our cash, spending a dollar here or five dollars there without a second thought. If you allow yourself to become conscious of what you are getting in return for what you are spending, you may decide to hold onto a few more of your dollars each week. Call this extra your "happiness money."

Next, ask yourself the bold question that my wise next-door neighbor, Mark, once asked me: "How much do you need to spend to be happy?" Set aside part of your happiness money for yourself, because until you have met your own needs, it is difficult to eagerly and joyously meet the needs of others.

Finally, take the remaining money and decide that with it you will make the world a better place. It truly doesn't matter how much or how little it is. As you could see from the story in this chapter, one single penny is enough to improve the countenance of another human being, because what we think about, believe in, and expect, we get. Whether it's several dollars or many dollars, money is energy that you can think of as fuel for life's engine. Look around your piece of the world, and you'll quickly know where to give or invest it for the highest good of all.

One last word on those pennies: I have a friend who lost her two-year-old son in a drowning accident several years ago. In his memory, she created "Michael's Pennies from Heaven," an online newsletter that shared stories from people around the world of finding pennies just when they needed them the most to lift a mood or provide comfort. Many of her readers saved their lucky pennies and asked what to do with them after they served their purpose. For a while, she ran "Penny Drives," in which people could send in their pennies toward a charitable cause. Although she is no longer publishing her newsletter, the hope and help she gave others continues to have a positive effect. Remember: Any amount is just the right amount to create wonders, if you're willing.

Flowers from David

The wonder of love that never dies

*M*ost people I know struggle with death. We hate being separated from those we love and wonder how we will ever get along without them. And while we're wondering if we will be okay, we also wonder if our deceased loved one is, too. The challenge is to realize that although bodies wear out or get hurt, love never dies and can keep us close in mind and spirit. How can we be sure of that? Let your heart make its wishes. You might be surprised when, someday, proof arrives that all is well.

MANY, MANY PEOPLE LOVED HARRIET, but David was her soul mate. Though there were twenty-two years between them, Harriet considered David, the son of her good friend Liza, to be her "birthday twin" since they shared the same birth date.

On June 14, 1999, Harriet and David celebrated their

birthdays together at a big bash given by his family. She was seventy-four that day; he turned fifty-two. But she would turn seventy-five without him because David died from cancer shortly after their party.

When the holidays rolled around that year, Harriet missed David. She believed he was with her beloved angels, but wished for his presence in her life anyway. She tried to stay busy around the house so she wouldn't think of him, but it was no use. He was on her mind and in her heart. As she allowed her memories to fill her with love, something wonderful happened.

The doorbell rang. There stood a messenger bearing flowers. The box was huge, with so many blossoms that Harriet needed not one but two vases to display them all. She delighted in their beauty, their ripe abundance, their grace. And when she opened the card, something even more wonderful happened.

It read: "Love, it is a flower and you are its only seed." It was signed, "David."

Harriet immediately called the florist. No, David had not ordered them in advance of his death. No, they had not been sent to her by his mother. They were from her friend Marilyn, but that was not the card that was supposed to accompany the bouquet. The florist was embarrassed because the card Harriet received was supposed to go with another delivery. He could not explain the mix-up.

But Harriet knew it was no mistake. "I truly think I received a message from David," she said later, "just when I needed it most."

☺ *Love Light: Angel Kisses*

An angel kiss is an instant of reassurance from beyond our earthly dimension that we are loved and that everything's okay. The wonder of angel kisses is that you never know where they will come from. They are often related to moments when you are missing someone you've lost, sweet proof that the love you shared in life survives death.

If you'd like to receive an angel kiss, try this simple exercise. Close your eyes. Take a few deep breaths, releasing both your physical tension and mental concerns. Just relax. Then think of someone you once loved who is now gone. Focus on someone with whom you shared a good relationship, not a contentious one or one that resulted in a breakup or divorce. Start with a name, and then allow your subconscious to bring a picture of this individual to your mind. Concentrate on this mental picture until the details come into focus. See the top of the person's head, then the forehead and eyes, then the nose, mouth, cheeks, and chin. Allow the body to take shape, and imagine that you are holding it. Remember this person's familiar smell and how it felt for the two of you to embrace.

Then listen as your loved one starts to speak. Hear the sound of his/her voice. You will likely hear something familiar. Mentally respond, as if you two were having a conversation. Allow the words to flow between you or a sweet silence if you didn't talk much when you were together. Enjoy the pleasure of being in your beloved's presence again. It is a scientific fact that our bodies don't know the difference between something we're merely thinking about and an actual experience of it, so while you are imagining your loved one, your experience is as "real" as if he or she were actually in the room with you.

After a minute or two of this, whisper, "Thanks," and open your eyes. This closes your prayer of the heart and lets all of heaven know that you would welcome more.

Then go about your business. Live your life. Expect something wonderful to happen. Like Harriet, you may get a message you never expected. You may hear "your song" on the radio. A friend might call and start talking about the deceased, bringing back memories you'd forgotten. You could find a memento you thought was lost for good. Or you might get a message in a dream. Keep your eyes, your ears, and your heart open and alert to wonder, never worrying about it, but always ready for it. You never know how the angels will connect the two of you again, but I assure you, they will. And that's wonderful.

God in Flight

The wonder of a sign of blessing

There are challenging times in life when we want reassurance. "Give me a sign," we say to God, rarely expecting that one will actually appear. And even if one does, most of us miss heavenly clues because they don't come in the form we expect or at the exact moment we're looking. Mostly, we think of signs as things that exist only in our fantasies. They're nice ideas, but not readily available.

That's because all too often we wish for signs when we are confused, frightened, or broken by life. It's hard to see miracles in the midst of misery. Rarely do we ask to see a sign just for the glory of it, the delight of proving that we are not alone and that all is well in the greater universe. Sometimes, when many, many people are secretly longing for a sign of God's blessing, one appears and everyone notices. That's what happened to the honorable George Sinner. I was at a conference where the former North Dakota governor told his story.

GOVERNOR SINNER WAS ATTENDING the Allied Tribes International Powwow as an honored guest. He was impressed with the costumes of the dancers, some of which were covered with eagle feathers, so he turned to his host and asked, "Isn't the eagle an endangered species? If your people believe in conservation, how can you use so many eagle feathers on your costumes?"

His host looked him in the eye and said, "You must understand that the eagle is sacred to our people. Those feathers have been handed down from generation to generation. If even one of them falls off a costume, the dancing will stop until it is retrieved and returned to its rightful owner."

Governor Sinner nodded. His host continued, "In fact, if an eagle were to fly over this gathering now, we would consider it a sign of God's blessing."

Governor Sinner looked around. They were on a flat plain outside the city limits of Bismarck, a highly developed area. There were no known eagle nesting places nearby. Although the sky was crystal blue that day, he had not seen many notable birds, much less an eagle.

But he wondered if any of the other 30,000 attendees were wishing, as he did, that an eagle would appear. It had been a peaceful gathering of people from across the United States. The event had been filled with goodwill and respect for all. Although he knew they had already been blessed by the abundant attendance and cooperation, he couldn't help but wonder how everyone there would feel if an eagle appeared. Was such a thing even possible near a densely populated urban area? He sat quietly in the stands, watching and wondering.

A few minutes later, something wonderful happened.

The drums stopped. The dancing stopped. And suddenly all eyes were peering up into the cloudless sky. For there, circling directly over the gathering, was not one eagle, but four. Governor Sinner knew that not only was the eagle sacred, but that in Indian lore, the four directions of north, east, south, and west were, too. Now here, in plain view for all to see, was not one but two unmistakable signs of blessing more powerful than anyone could have imagined.

"In spite of the size of the crowd, there was absolute silence," Governor Sinner said reverently. "No one moved until the eagles finally flew away. Then there was great rejoicing."

♡ *Love Light: Signs of Wonder*

There are signs of wonder around us every day. But we rarely notice them because our attention is not on where we are at the moment, but where we are not. We drive down the street stewing over the unfinished work we left on our desks. We walk through a mall concentrating on the product we want to find, not the stores or the people who are around us as we go. We carry on conversations like tacticians, focusing more on what we're going to say next than on what is being said and felt at the moment.

So if you want to see a sign, the first thing you must do is believe one is possible. If you do, then ask for what you need. Be specific about what you'd like the sign to be—a blessing on an action or event, a direction you should follow, reassurance that everything will be all right, or simply an indication that God exists and all is well. Make your request by speaking it out loud, not because heaven can't read your mind but because whenever we hear something "from the horse's mouth," so to speak, we believe it. In addition, speaking your request aloud creates a vibration of sound that is invisible to humans, but highly magnetic to energy in other fields of existence.

Something Wonderful Is About to Happen . . .

Once you've made your request, go about your business, but keep your eyes, ears, and heart open. Something wonderful *will* happen. Allow it to come to you in its own way and time. It probably won't happen immediately, but you may not have to wait very long. Anecdotal evidence from people who have asked for signs suggests that they often appear very quickly, within a day or two. Focus on your hope, not your worry, lack, or pain, and know the answer you seek is on its way.

The Hug

The wonder of sibling love

You sometimes hear stories about one sibling doing something extraordinary for another. An older brother will donate a kidney so his younger brother can quit dialysis. A girl will dive fully clothed into an icy lake to save her sister from drowning. Usually, these are conscious decisions made by children or young adults old enough to fully understand the possible consequences of their actions.

Only rarely do you hear a story like the one you are about to read, in which babies somehow help each other in a way that saves one of their lives. When one comes along, it's wonderful.

DALE WAS THE MOTHER OF THREE healthy children, ages four, two, and one. She loved children, and when she became pregnant for a fourth time, she was excited. Unfortunately, the newest pregnancy didn't go as well as had the first three. At three months, Dale started hemorrhaging, and her doctor recommended a D & C, a procedure that would have terminated the pregnancy.

Before Dale decided, she insisted on an ultrasound, which showed that she was carrying not one baby, but two. "I was delighted that I wasn't going to lose one baby, but was going to have two," she says. At that moment, the sense that everything was somehow going to be okay came over her; and against her doctor's strong suggestion, she refused the medical procedure. However, she agreed with her doctor that carrying the pregnancy to term would be extremely challenging. At only 4'11", Dale's tiny frame was not built for the strain of carrying two babies. And with three other small children at home, she would be hard-pressed to follow her doctor's order for six months of total bed rest.

Dale did the best she could. Her husband would dress the children in the morning and place all of them on the floor. From there, Dale could diaper, feed, and play with them without ever having to pick them up. "I would let them hug me whenever they wanted," she said, "but it really was difficult trying to keep up with all three."

Even being careful, Dale kept having contractions. She was in and out of the hospital frequently, where the doctors managed to stop the contractions until finally her blood pressure could take no more of the medication. Her twins, Riley and Carly, were born seven and a half weeks early.

Dale, allergic to local anesthetics, had a cesarean section under general anesthesia. A day passed before she learned that Carly was okay, but that Riley had taken a breath too soon and had gotten amniotic fluid in her lungs. The doctors had resuscitated Riley and rushed her off into a special isolated unit. For the first time, the identical twins were separated.

Although Carly dropped down to two and a half pounds, she went into the nursery with the other babies. Her body temperature was holding, and she was able to eat. But Riley struggled. She went into an incubator, but her condition did not improve.

The family's pediatrician was very supportive. Dale was extremely upset over Riley's condition, so he encouraged Dale to take Carly home and resume a normal family life as soon as possible. Although she was an experienced mother, nothing had prepared Dale for life with a premature baby. "I was afraid to change Carly's diaper," she admits, "because it was like changing diapers on a Barbie doll. And while I wanted my children to be part of everything with their new sister, I couldn't allow them to pick her up because she was so tiny. Preemies don't know how to take a bottle, so you have to hold their tongue down and rub their cheeks to get them to suck. So I would hold down her tongue and let the kids rub her cheeks."

In spite of her best efforts, Dale admits, "It was horrible. I was still trying to recover from the C-section, take care of my other children, and I was emotionally devastated having to leave one 'behind.' My husband would spend most of the day at the hospital with Riley. After the first week, I tried to go up to the hospital to see her, too; but I was in denial about how bad things really were."

Indeed, Riley's condition was worsening. She often stopped breathing when she fell asleep and so was attached to monitors that would rouse her if necessary. She had a feeding tube because she didn't have the strength to eat. Even with that, she was spitting up whatever she was given. "It was as if she didn't have the desire to be nourished," Dale says. When Riley was two and a half weeks old, Dale and her husband received a phone call saying that the doctors could not find a medical reason that Riley could not hold food. In addition, her breathing was stopping often. Because of this, the doctors said they would have to transfer her to a critical care children's hospital, although the outlook was grim.

The family's pediatrician said they were going to transfer Riley the next morning. But then suddenly he asked an interesting question: "Have you ever been depressed? What is it like for you?"

"Well, I don't eat," Dale said, "and I don't sleep well, either." When she recognized the same symptoms in her daughter, Dale's immediate thought was that Riley missed her since she had only had minimal visits to the hospital.

"No," the doctor said. "I think she needs her sister. She's only seen Carly once since birth. Let's try an experiment. Bring Carly to the hospital and let's see how Riley reacts."

Dale and her husband immediately hopped in the car and took Carly to the hospital. And that's when something wonderful happened. "We put Carly in the incubator with Riley," Dale says. "Riley was lying on her back, all hooked up to machines. Carly lay on her side and looked at Riley. Then she put her little hand on her sister's belly."

Dale started crying. "The minute Carly touched Riley's belly, the weight of fear lifted from me, and I knew everything was going to be okay," she says. The nurses and doctors were stunned. "It was like Carly knew that her sister needed her touch," Dale says. The doctor asked if Carly could stay overnight, and Dale and her husband agreed. "I thought, omygod, they are so connected," she says. "I felt bad that I hadn't brought Carly up sooner. At that moment, I realized babies do feel love and have knowledge."

The next morning, something even more wonderful happened. "I got a call from a very excited nurse," Dale explains. "She said, 'We just turned off the heater, and Riley's temperature stayed up.' " The girls stayed together; and by the end of the day, Dale's husband gave Riley her first bottle. She held down the food.

Wonderfully, both girls came home the following morning. "Within forty-eight hours of being with her sister, all of Riley's vital signs improved," Dale says, "and she never had a relapse." The girls have been inseparable ever since. Now ten years old, they are always together. Although they have two beds in their room, they usually share the same bed. If one of them tries to sneak away, the other wakes up. When their school system insisted the girls be separated, Carly developed a reading problem. Once the girls were reunited, the problem disappeared.

Dale's perspective has been changed forever by the experience. "I believe that as humans we need each other more than we'd like to admit," she says. "We draw healing energy from each other, especially from love and touch. The lesson is that we need to be there emotionally, spiritually, and physically for one another. I also have come to believe that babies are real people within those little bodies with genuine feelings, emotions, and needs."

Carly now says, "There's no difference between me and my sister." Riley adds, "The only way to tell us apart is our hair."

Two lives; one indestructible bond. Wonderful.

♥ *Love Light: Gut Instincts*

No one told Carly what to do when she was placed in the bassinet with her sister. No one manipulated her or made her do what she did. Somehow, she just knew.

So do you. The next time you know someone needs you, go to him or her. When you get there, listen to your gut, not your intellect. No matter what is going on, you will know what to do next.

That may be nothing. At least, nothing that involves taking

action. Sometimes the greatest gift one human can give another is to simply be present and truly see them, not their medical condition. There is no way to know what Carly saw when she looked at her sister or what she felt or thought at that moment. There is also no way to be sure whether Riley simply sensed her sister's presence or whether Carly's "hug" made the difference. All that the family knows is that neither Dale's nor her husband's attention helped nearly as much as one connection with Carly.

You likely know at least one other person instinctively. You need no words to understand each other. And you know, in spite of debilitating medical conditions or other troubles, who that person really is and what he or she needs. Go and be a witness to love. For when you do, it's wonderful.

Shadow Boxing

The wonder of seeing things differently

When we fall in love, our world becomes wonderful. Ordinary things shimmer with a sparkle that only the glow of love can provide. But eventually that light casts shadows, and we can see that there is a back side to radiance, which is that it can become boring, tedious, or frustrating. This is especially true when we're tired, hungry, overworked, or annoyed.

Love and honor mean one thing when we commit to one another and quite another after a long day at work or after a night without sleep. When that happens, anything goes. Or rather, everything does. Where is the light of happiness, hope, and contentment when we need it the most? Ironically, it is closer than we think. This story took place several years ago, but it still holds true.

AT 5:30 P.M., I OPENED THE DOOR to the kitchen, stepped inside, and sighed. My daughters' remnants from hours of play lay abandoned across every horizontal surface, a land mine of waxy crayons, primary-colored plastic, Barbie doll gear, and other assorted toy pieces. Hadn't I asked—with a "please"—for them to put the toys away before I got home? A pile of dirty dishes lay rotting in the sink, although nothing was cooking for supper. I glanced at the clock: less than one hour until the girls had to be at ballet lessons. No time for the nap I craved. Barely time to cook and eat. No time to relax before I tackled the article I had to write on deadline. How could I do it all?

I needed Support and went looking for him. Steve, my husband and partner of a dozen years. Steve, my beloved friend who never let me down. Steve, who was now sound asleep on the living-room couch, taking my nap.

"Thanks a lot!" I grumbled angrily as I shook him to consciousness.

"Whaaa . . . what'd I do?"

I smacked him with sarcasm. "Thanks for picking up and starting dinner!"

He started to close his eyes once more. "I thought we could go out for fast food . . ."

"We've eaten that stuff three times this week already! Why couldn't you put on a pot of pasta?"

He sat up and tried to steady himself by placing both feet on the floor. "Okay. You want me to do that now?"

I stormed out of the room. "*No!* I'll do it! Don't let me disturb you!" I turned to the stairs. "Girls!" I hollered. "Get down here and pick up your junk!"

I went into the kitchen and started to take serious action. I banged cupboard doors. Cursed under my breath. Slammed pots down on the stove. Kicked toys into a corner. I could feel my face getting red, my blood pressure rising. "Nobody ever does anything to help around here," I grumbled as I worked. "I can't do everything. There just aren't enough hours in the day." Despite the adrenaline rush from my anger, I started to feel weary with frustration.

The girls ran into the room but quickly departed when they saw my bad mood. I barely noticed. A cloud of gloom that even the sunniest smiles wouldn't have been able to penetrate had settled in.

I sat stone-faced through dinner, determined to spread my misery to others. Although Steve cleared the table and did the dishes, there was no turning back from my condemnation.

"I can take the kids to ballet," he offered.

"No, you can't," I snapped. "You have to do the dishes."

I drove in silence, my fists becoming white-knuckled as I clenched the steering wheel. I started to feel dizzy. Suddenly, it came to me in a flash: I didn't want to feel this way. No, more than that—I didn't want to *be* this way. What happened to the loving wife and mother? Where was the woman with endless patience and energy? Could something as simple as clutter and spaghetti really change my personality so dramatically?

I tried telling myself that everything was okay, that everything would be all right, but my body and my emotions wouldn't respond to what my head was saying. I dropped off the girls, calling "I love you!" after them, although I doubted at that moment that they believed me.

As I drove away, I tried a different stress-release exercise. Since positive thinking wasn't working, I decided to go with my negative rampage rather than fight it. I had already identified the thought that I didn't want to feel angry and upset. Now came the hard part: I had to hear myself say it. I cleared my throat, took a deep breath, and barely whispered: "I don't want to feel this way."

I felt my hands relax a bit, so I tried again, this time with more conviction.

"I don't want to feel this way!"

I felt like I was in a football stadium, and the cheerleaders were hollering, "We can't hear you!" So I sat up straighter and launched the words with gusto.

"I don't want to feel this way!"

At that moment, something wonderful happened. I started to laugh at myself, and I relaxed. I realized how ridiculous I had been sounding and acting all evening and had flashbacks to how silly I must have looked to my family as I banged around the kitchen. I realized that my fatigue and stress had been talking all evening, not my common sense. And since I didn't want to feel that way, I could choose something better.

My imagination then took me back to the living room, remembering Steve sleeping on the couch. With the spell of my anger broken, I could see that he was simply a tired guy who flopped on the first inviting piece of furniture not with malicious intent, but simply because he, like me, was exhausted. Suddenly, I could see myself saying, "Good idea," cuddling up next to him, and falling asleep. We could have rested for a while, then awakened to order pizza for dinner. It wouldn't have been a three-course meal, but at least it was nutritious, acceptable under the circumstances.

With a change of perspective, I saw the clutter and mess differently, too. The toys were evidence of our children's joy and creativity. Looking through refreshed eyes, I could see how my little beloveds had spent their day.

When I saw things differently, Steve was neither the hero

nor the villain. I was—or rather, my negative thoughts were. By choosing to pay attention to all that was annoying, worrying, or upsetting me, all I got was annoyed, worried, and upset. When I changed my focus, the change in my feelings—and my body— was unexpectedly wonderful. I felt like myself and was ready to go home and try again, this time enjoying, not verbally and emotionally destroying, what was mine. And somehow I knew that the next time I was exhausted or upset, I would try to see myself and my day in a better light before I covered my family with shadows.

I walked back in the house. Steve had finished the dishes and picked up the toys. Now he was back on the couch, reading a magazine. I walked over and gave him a hug.

"Thanks," I said.

"For what?"

I laughed. "Ignoring me."

He laughed, too. "You're tired. C'mere," he said, moving to one side so I could stretch out next to him. I settled in. It felt wonderful to be home.

⑤ *Love Light: Happy Endings*

Every day, we do terrible damage to our lives by what we say to ourselves. Of the 50,000 thoughts we have every day, 80 percent are negative and an astonishing 95 percent are a repeat of what we thought yesterday! The destructive monologue goes on in our brains all day, every day. "I can't get to that"; "I don't want this to happen"; "No one ever pays any attention to what I think"; "I never get what I want." Can't, don't, no one, never, not, isn't, should, ought . . . There's no end to how we deny ourselves the happiness we seek by always expecting the worst.

One of the ways to make something wonderful happen is to break the chain of negativity. This is not always easy to do when you are angry or upset. As you could see, positive thinking wasn't getting me anywhere, because I didn't believe it. Instead, you can try what I did. Go with the flow by using your "nots" to untie the knots in your perception. Say out loud: *I don't want to feel this way anymore!* Do it over and over until you feel a shift in your body and perspective.

If that doesn't work, try a variation on the children's game called "I spy through my little eyes." You remember how it goes: You're driving down the street, and you look for something that starts with the letter A, then the letter B, then C, D, and so on. Or you look for an object that's a particular color, shape, or size. In this case, try, "I spy through my little eyes something that makes me feel better right now." You might notice the way the light comes through a window or a cat curled contentedly in an old easy chair. Keep playing, looking for proof that everything's okay right where you are. As in the exercise above, repeat until you feel something switch inside, like a train moving over to a new track. You'll know you've done this when you feel calmer, safer, more relaxed. Once the pressure is off, you can take action that is more in line with your better intentions and character.

Shed some light on your shadows; for when you do, you are likely to see that what you want or need in that moment is right in front of you. That's when wonderful things start to happen.

You Never Know

The wonder of nonjudgment

*Y*ou hear it every day: "What terrible news! I'm so sorry to hear that." Or, "How wonderful! You must be thrilled!" We are quick to judge the events that happen to us and others as either good or bad. Once they are labeled, we cut off the possibility that they could be anything else. But sometimes, "bad" events are really blessings in disguise and "good" ones bring pain and trouble in their wake. If we truly want something wonderful to happen, we must wait to see the results of an event before we snap to judgment, as this *Midrash* (parable) suggests.

THERE ONCE WAS A RABBI who had one son. They lived together in a small village and raised horses. One day, the son came running into the house, breathless and upset.

"Father, Father!" he cried. "I accidentally left the corral open last night, and all the horses escaped!"

The rabbi barely looked up from the book he was reading. "Could be a good thing; could be a bad thing. You never know."

The next day, the son again ran into his father's study, this time agitated with excitement.

"Father, Father! Our horses are back, and they have brought a herd of wild mustangs with them!"

Again, the rabbi was nonplussed. "Could be a good thing; could be a bad thing. You never know."

The son was surprised at his father's lack of reaction, but continued his work with the animals. A few days later, he was thrown while trying to tame one of the wild stallions and broke his leg. Although his son was in pain, the father was calm. "Could be a good thing; could be a bad thing. You never know," he said.

The next week, an army of Cossacks came into town. They conscripted every able-bodied young man except the rabbi's son, who lay in bed healing.

The soldiers left them in peace, which was wonderful. After they had gone, the rabbi went to his son. "You see? Could be a good thing; could be a bad thing. You never know," he said with a smile.

♥ *Love Light: Wait and See*

The next time you hear news that you might otherwise judge as good or bad, try playing the game of "How interesting!" No matter what the other person says, you simply respond, "How interesting! Tell me more." He or she may spill his/her heart to you, to which you can offer a smile, a hug, or a tear, depending upon what is appropriate. Instead of getting all caught up in another person's emotional state, stay relatively neutral, wondering what might come next.

If you do, you will likely find that things are neither as bad—nor as good—as they may first appear. Lottery winners may have financial problems; terminal patients may improve or sometimes even get well.

Life is very, very interesting. There is always something wonderful happening.

It's Good to Be Queen!

The wonder of acting "as if"

Most of us are afraid to change our roles. It is challenging to see ourselves in a new light and even harder to get others to see us that way. We believe what we perceive; so if we look in the mirror and see something less than wonderful, we are likely to be disappointed by others.

This is never more true than when we'd like to win an award or receive a promotion. In order for these wonderful things to happen, other people must view us in a very special light. This starts not so much with them, but with us. First, we must see ourselves differently. Then we must act as if the new thing we want is possible, which is never easy, since the human mind has difficulty imagining something it has not already experienced.

But if we can imagine, great wonders can happen.

AMANDA WAS GOING TO THE PROM. But she wasn't content to simply attend it; she wanted to reign over it.

"I want to be prom queen, Mom," she said calmly one morning at breakfast.

Although Amanda was pretty and popular, I knew the competition was formidable and didn't think she should set her heart on winning the crown. "You'll have a great time no matter what happens," I said. "Why don't you just relax and enjoy being with your friends?"

"Because I want to be the queen," she said matter-of-factly.

The next day, I found her in her room, wearing a tiara from a fairy princess costume she had as a child. She was making faces in the mirror.

"What are you doing?" I asked.

"Practicing my prom queen smile," she said. "What do you think?"

"Looks good," I said, admiring her confidence. "Keep it up."

As the days went on, the fake tiara appeared more and more. Sometimes she wore it with a towel or blanket, mimicking a queen's robe. When she had it on, Amanda sat up straighter and looked us in the eye more often. Her voice was clear and strong. Very regal.

Steve and I didn't know what to say. We had tried to encourage both of our daughters to always go for their dreams, but we usually focused on ones that were within their control, not ones based on someone else's opinions. As much as we both wanted to see Amanda get the title and the crown, we didn't want to give her any false hopes nor put a pin in the balloon of her dreams. So mostly we kept quiet.

Over the course of the next few weeks, there was little doubt that something in our daughter had shifted, and she now regarded herself as the queen. She wasn't arrogant about it. On the contrary, she seemed to be completely at peace with the idea that she would rule the dance.

Still, when we said good-bye to her and her date on prom night, we smiled through gritted teeth. "I'm not sure I can bear to see her face when she comes home," I said. "I just hope she has a good time."

Then something wonderful happened.

When she walked in the door shortly after midnight, it wasn't her smile but the glittering tiara on her head that caught my eye first. "Guess what!" she exclaimed, grinning from ear to ear. She didn't have to finish the sentence. Her eyes sparkled with energy. She was not the least bit tired from the hours of dancing and partying. We both gave her a big hug. "Congratulations, Sweetheart!"

She wore the tiara to breakfast the next day, and the next, and the next. Amanda saw herself as she wanted to be; and as she did, apparently others did, too. And I saw that the little girl I had always tried to protect from disappointment was now a young woman with the confidence to make wonderful things happen.

♥ Love Light: Playdreaming

We did it as children, but most of us are out of practice. Playdreaming. It's the art of pretending that we are, have, or can do whatever our hearts most desire.

Playdreaming does something that no amount of positive thinking or affirming ever will: It helps us "walk our talk." Words are reflective of good intentions; but until our actions bring them to life, they are nothing more than abstract ideas.

Here's how to do it: Decide something you want to be or have or do. Make it something that you have never been or owned or done before, and the game will be much more fun. Be specific. Don't say, "I want to be happier." That's too vague. Say, "I want to be a skydiver."

Once you've made your choice, start gathering information. Read skydiving magazines. Start talking the language of skydivers as if you already are one and are part of that group of people. Look at photographs and watch movies of skydivers so you can get a mental picture of what happens during a jump. If you have the time and are geographically close to a skydiving center, go spend a day there, watching, listening, and learning.

Keep a journal, and every night, write in your pretend adventures as a skydiver. You can put things like, "Made my first jump today with my instructor. I was terrified, but I couldn't believe the feeling of freedom. Loved it!" Make the feeling come alive with your words.

Once a day, every day, close your eyes and allow the feeling of making a successful jump to surge through your veins. If you're out of shape, start exercising. If you lack funds, start saving your pennies and nickels in a jar. In other words, get used to being the very thing you say you want to be.

Playdreaming allows us to feel how we will feel once our dream is achieved. It takes away our resistance to what we want, builds up our positive belief that it is possible, and encourages others to see us as we would like to see ourselves. Playdreaming is fun, harmless, and easy to do. Start by thinking about a goal you'd like to accomplish, then follow the process to make your dreams come alive. Once you are in the right frame of mind, wonderful things are more likely to enter your life.

The Biggest Barbecue

The wonder of extraordinary generosity

*E*veryone has a heart, but some people have extraordinarily big ones. They are always the first to arrive at the door with a casserole when a friend is sick. They never hesitate when someone asks for a dollar or an hour of time or a sympathetic ear. It seems as if they have a bottomless well of love that never runs dry. When tragedy strikes, they are the people who always seem to know what to say or do to make things better. I've been fortunate to know several people like this in my lifetime, but never before had I met someone with a heart big enough to hold an entire city. That is, until I met Texas Lil.

IN APRIL 1997, A MASSIVE FLOOD devastated our region. More than 60,000 people were affected. Thousands of homes, as well as businesses, schools, and churches, were damaged or destroyed.

Many, many people lost everything they had worked for all their lives. And those who didn't were physically, mentally, emotionally, and spiritually weary from trying to recover what they had left. It was a dark and dreary time.

Then in May, something wonderful happened. Texas Lil came to town. She was the ray of sunshine we so desperately needed. A dude ranch owner from Justin, Texas, Lil was the proud owner and operator of the World's Largest Transportable Smoker, a 57-foot semi that could cook enough beef brisket to feed 10,000 people at once. She decided that the people of our town needed a decent dinner, and she was right. Few of us had more than a trickle of water to our homes, and that wasn't safe to drink. Even fewer had electricity or gas for cooking. Almost all the restaurants in town were still closed, and most peoples' outdoor barbecue grills floated upriver. Most meals consisted of either cold sandwiches or casseroles from the Red Cross or Salvation Army trucks.

But Lil changed all that. She pulled into town with the thirty-six-foot smokestack of her "super-smoker" scenting the air with an inviting barbecue aroma for miles around. She parked it on the University of North Dakota campus and invited everyone from our sister cities of Grand Forks, North Dakota, and East Grand Forks, Minnesota, to supper.

When she did, something wonderful happened. The Boy Scouts gathered potatoes from area farmers and somehow got them baked. The few area grocers who had reopened donated cups, plates, forks, and knives. One of the fast-food chains donated enough orange drink to float the *Titanic*. The University of North Dakota opened its football stadium, one of the few campus properties that hadn't sustained heavy damage. The sun peeked out and the people arrived, thousands upon thousands.

Texas Lil, the hostess supreme, stood outside the stadium that night. She was utterly resplendent in a turquoise fringed skirt, snap-buttoned blouse, and the whitest cowboy hat I'd ever seen. Even the steel toes of her boots were gleaming—a rarity in a town covered in mud. We all tried to clean up as best we could, but those of us in the long, snaking lines heading into the stadium were a ragtag bunch. We wore our cleanest jeans and the least mud-covered sweatshirts we could find and carried good appetites.

Although the lines were long and slow, no one complained. Texas Lil greeted each and every one of us, offering her big-as-Texas grin and a hug for those who wanted one. Blessings and thanks colored her exchanges; her love for total strangers was totally authentic. I heard her say more than once that she wished she could do more for us, although it was hard to imagine what that might be since she had already done the impossible: brought us together and made us smile again.

The mood was bright inside the stadium. For the first time in the weeks since the disaster, children ran and played on the football field, totally free from their parents' constant warnings to stay away from dangerous places. Adults who had not seen each other since the evacuation sat in the bleachers and swapped stories. There were hugs and tears. One of the local radio stations played loud music, but we all loved it. It was our first party since the flood, and it was a great one.

I have a postcard from that night. On it is a picture of Texas Lil's semi. I can still smell the brisket smoking and taste the barbecue sauce in my mouth. But mostly I remember her smile, her warm and genuine "Howdy!" and her wonderful willingness to drive halfway across the country just to give thousands of people supper. She did it for love, not for money. No one put her name in lights or across the front of a building. But those of us who were there that night will forever hold her kindness in our hearts.

❂ *Love Light: Dishing Up Love*

Although you may not have the means or the desire to feed the masses, you can serve up a meal full of love anywhere, anytime. Simply pick the food that you do best, even if it's pizza or hot dogs. Then bring it forth with all the gusto you can muster. Add music, candlelight, or starlight. Invite your favorite person or people. Serve yourself last so you can watch and revel in your guests' delight.

In every culture all around the world, shared food is a pathway to personal and communal peace. As Lil showed us that night, that can happen even in the wake of a disaster. But no matter when it takes place, it's wonderful.

Beautiful Hands

The wonder of self-acceptance

*W*ho among us does not dread the hazards of old age? Even if our minds remain sharp, our bodies can become traitorous. Like errant children, they willfully disobey our commands, refusing to move as fast or as well as we would like. Even if all the parts still work well, they may nonetheless make us look older than we feel. Like it or not, they are still ours, and we must live with them, hopefully in peace. This is not always easy. But when you can see your body differently, wonderful things can happen.

"PLACE YOUR HAND PALM DOWN on a piece of paper," I said to my seminar group. "Then draw around the outside, going around each finger." The room full of adult women giggled as their pencils and pens traced the contours of their hands. "Now draw in the nails, and any veins, lines, and spots that you may have,"

I said. "It's fine to add wrinkles and chapped or calloused places, too. Just draw your hands as they are at this time of your life."

What had started out as tickled laughter soon turned to the silence of concern and disapproval. "Don't worry about how your hands look," I said, knowing that a woman's vanity is often tied up with her hands' appearance. I thought of Scarlett O'Hara visiting Rhett Butler in jail, hoping to fool him into thinking that all was well at her Tara plantation and knowing that her hands would give her away as someone who had been digging in the fields in order to survive. There are times when we wish our hands would not betray us. From the sound of things, for some of the people in the room, this was one of those times.

"Now, write a few sentences about the story your hands tell about you," I suggested. "They are a biography of the places you've been and the things you've done. Let them speak."

Everyone in the room started writing except Marge.* I knew she had arthritis and thought that perhaps she was experiencing pain or discomfort holding her pen. "Do you hurt?" I whispered. "You can just think about it. Don't feel you have to do this exercise if you don't want to."

She shook her head. I couldn't tell if she was saying no to doing the exercise or no to the question about pain. I turned and walked back to the front of the room to give her some space.

After a minute, I could see that Marge was writing. Her head was bent over her work and she was concentrating deeply. I wanted to go over and peek at what she was writing because it was obviously intense, but I just stayed in the front of the room until I saw that many of the women had put down their pens and were ready to share what they had written. Most talked about the wonderful memories they saw in their hands—all the good times their hands had brought them in the past.

*Name has been changed.

Finally, it was Marge's turn. "Do you want to read yours to the group?" I asked. "You don't have to unless you want to."

Again, she shook her head. "No, I don't think so," she said. I was just about to turn to the next person when I heard her voice again. "Okay. I will."

She cleared her throat and sat up a little straighter, although she kept her eyes on her paper. "I hate my hands," she began. "The knuckles are too big and they hurt. The veins are ugly, and my hands won't always do what I want them to do."

We all sat in a pool of silence for a moment, feeling her pain. And then something wonderful happened. She started to smile, and her voice changed from harsh to soft. Her body relaxed, and the words poured out.

"But these are the hands that can still splash cool water on my face on a hot summer's day. These are the hands that clean my body and make my bed. These are the hands that caress my loved ones and help me hold them."

She looked up, made eye contact with one of the women near her, and said confidently, "I love my beautiful hands!"

I glanced around the room and could see that some of the women were crying. I was holding back tears myself. I thought about how often I had dismissed one of my own body parts as inadequate or less than what I hoped. Marge showed us that true beauty lies not in appearances, but in acceptance and appreciation.

Now, when my nails break or my veins stick out because I've been typing too much or my skin gets chapped because I've helped my daughter unstick her car door in February, I bless my hands. Marge was right. They're wonderful.

❧ *Love Light: Embracing Beauty*

Although every society has its own standards of beauty, few venerate the visual reports of disease or decay that our bodies sometimes manifest. But maybe it's time to change that and see our physical forms through kinder, more unconditionally loving eyes.

I once read that our bodies are the biography of our lives, revealing every thought, fear, or encounter we've ever had. Besides their value as revealers of truth, our bodies are incredibly sturdy, carrying on in spite of the mental and physical abuse we often give them. We feed them poorly, work them overtime, starve them of sleep. It's amazing—and wonderful—that they continue to work as well as they do.

Today, pick a body part you've never particularly liked. Try to see beyond its appearance and ask, "What have you done for me in the past?" or "What can you do for me now?" If you can't bring yourself to do that, try using one of your body parts that you *do* like. Appreciate how strong, flexible, or healthy it is. Don't go beyond your limits—just enjoy whatever you can comfortably do without stress or strain. You might surprise yourself by discovering that in spite of how things look, all really is wonderful with you.

The Sweetest Kiss

The wonder of a child's love

Children do not see disabilities or other outward physical appearances the way adults do. While we become accustomed to accepting—or, more accurately, rejecting—one another at face value, children only look for love. It is amazing how often they find it, in spite of the face we present to them. When a child perceives the good in an adult, wonderful things happen.

It was Christmas. Kathy and her husband, Randy, elders in their urban church, went to pray and celebrate. Their congregation was both small and unique, including some homeless and some drug-addicted people. Kathy and Randy's five children accompanied them, including their youngest, six-year-old Josiah.

Josiah is a very special child. At age three, he was diagnosed with an inoperable brain cancer; and before he was five, he nearly died. At one point, Josiah was so disfigured by his disease that he was nearly unrecognizable except to those who knew and loved him best. Yet he not only survived, but was approaching his seventh birthday disease-free. If there was anything the family had learned, it was that people are not always as they appear.

That night, as the congregation was gathering, Josiah was approached by an alcoholic named Ricky. Kathy says that Ricky's appearance can be off-putting, since he is emaciated and toothless. Alcohol has destroyed both his liver and his looks, and he appears much older than he is. His words are often slurred, and he is slow to move and to speak.

Ricky came over to Josiah and asked, "Can I shake your hand? Merry Christmas, little buddy." Josiah raised his eyes to meet Ricky's and raised up his arms for a hug rather than a handshake. Ricky was clearly touched as he bent down to receive Josiah's embrace. After a few precious moments, Ricky pulled away.

Then something wonderful happened.

As Ricky began to straighten up, Josiah said, "Wait!" Josiah reached up, grabbed Ricky's neck, and pulled Ricky down close to his face. Then he kissed Ricky's cheek firmly. Ricky's smile turned to tears of joy, and he walked away with a rare quickness.

"To me, Josiah's kiss represented the unconditional love of God," Kathy said. "That extra kiss He gives us is sometimes the only beautiful thing in our lives and may be the very thing that gets us through. My prayer is that everyone would recognize the 'Kiss of God' in their lives and relish it for all it's worth."

☺ *Love Light: Little Wonders*

Children love to love and be loved. So if you are lucky enough to have a small child in your life, go give him or her a hug right now.

You are practically guaranteed of getting one right back.

If you do not have a little one in your life, think about yourself as a young child. If you came from an affectionate family, choose a happy memory and relive it. If your family was cold and critical, close your eyes and give the "little you" the hug you always wanted.

Doing these things may not change your life, but they will change your mind. For love is where we perceive it to be. Mostly we keep it hidden by fear about our self-worth or whether or not we'd be doing the right thing by expressing it. Children have no such inhibitions until we tell them they must develop them. Drop yours and give love a chance. It's a wonderful thing to try.

Working for the Love of It

The wonder of a heartfelt decision

*M*ost businesspeople know how to make a good decision. They take the facts that are presented to them, play them against what they know from their experience, and choose a course of action that aligns what they believe to be possible with what they want.

Sometimes, however, that tried-and-true formula doesn't work. This is especially so when other people are involved. They bring their own sets of wants, beliefs, and needs to the decision-making process. At that point, either the loudest voice wins or a compromise is negotiated. But what happens when neither the voice of reason nor the screams of fear win? Even the most seemingly ordinary business transaction can become special when we make room for wonder.

Something Wonderful Is About to Happen . . .

ISABEL* IS A LITERARY AGENT who knows about more than books. She knows spirit. She keeps on her desk a box of 150 spiritual affirmations given to her by a friend and contemplates one each day before she starts her work. Sometimes they urge her to take action: "I take nothing for granted," says one, which coaxes her to count her blessings or send off a note of thanks. Other times, they reflect the better parts of her personality, making her glad that she honors her integrity: "I use my time well; I enjoy being productive." Isabel often finds that the slice of inspiration she picks at random often reflects something she wants to do or needs to think about. Choosing her morning affirmation is like hearing her intuition say, "Wake up to this!" She takes the messages lightheartedly, always wondering what coincidence might occur that reflects the line she has received for that day.

One day, she lifted "I am a loyal and compassionate friend" from the box. She wasn't planning to see any friends that day, so she was curious as to how the affirmation might relate to the experiences she believed were ahead.

Later that morning, without advance notice, a friend of hers dropped by the office. Although Isabel preferred not to mix business with friendship and had never sold a piece of literary fiction, she had agreed weeks before to represent this woman's work. As long as her friend had dropped in, Isabel took the opportunity to present the advantages and disadvantages of each of the publishing houses to which she had submitted the manuscript. She didn't make recommendations about which house she thought was best. Thinking, "I am a loyal and compassionate friend," she waited for her friend to give the project direction, since ultimately the decision could affect their friendship.

Much to Isabel's surprise, the woman was the most enthusiastic about a small publisher Isabel liked, but who would only

*Name has been changed.

offer a modest advance for her friend's work. "I feel it's where I need to be," the author said. Thinking "I am a loyal and compassionate friend," Isabel set aside her own business instinct to seek a large advance and told her friend she would support her in whatever she wanted to do.

Acting strictly from the heart, Isabel picked up the phone and called the editor to tell her of the writer's decision. "Tell her to wait!" the editor exclaimed. "I'll be right there!"

The editor flew out of her building, hopped into a taxi, and rushed breathlessly into Isabel's office. The trio talked for over an hour; and when the editor left, Isabel called the other publishers and told them not to make any offers since it looked like they would make a deal. It was the right thing to do. She felt satisfied. She knew she had both a happy editor and a happy writer/friend, even though her commission would be minuscule.

And then something wonderful happened.

The editor called a short time later to say that the publisher had decided to make the book the lead on their fall list, a very prestigious placement. "The most amazing thing was that the book was a collection of short stories, which would not normally get that kind of attention," Isabel said. The editor said they were rushing catalog copy to the printer the very next day so they could announce the book quickly. Both the editor and the publisher said they were totally committed to making the book work, which would ultimately mean strong sales and income for the writer, the publisher, and ultimately Isabel as the agent.

"Good things will happen with this book," Isabel said later. "I honored my friend's wishes and thought about what was best for her. Sometimes you just have to have faith and believe."

❂ *Love Light: From the Heart*

It's difficult to override the workings of our often overactive minds. Although we try to use reason, sometimes it works against rather than for us.

That's why, like Isabel, I keep a "Wonder Box" on my desk. It's filled with affirmations about what is true or what I want to be true about me as a person and about my life. I wrote the affirmations myself, sitting at my computer with closed eyes and an open heart. Whatever came out of my mind, I typed. When I opened my eyes, I cleaned up the spelling errors, printed out the pages, and cut them into strips, like the sayings found in fortune cookies. Then I folded each one lovingly in half and dropped it in the box.

It is astonishing how often the words resonate with something I have been thinking and feeling but have been unable to express. Sometimes the wonder statements remind me of something I have forgotten. Other times, they nudge me to take action. I always see them as gifts of the spirit from the larger, wiser part of me to the smaller, more distracted one. When I believe the words and apply them to my life, wonderful things happen.

Here are twenty of my favorite affirmations. Write your own, or use these to start your own Wonder Box. Write them on small strips of paper, fold them in half, and pick one at random every day before you begin work. Read it out loud, and think about what it means to you. Then set it down and go about your work. You'll be surprised at how often a wonderful "coincidence" will show up!

My life is on the right track. I am achieving the things I want. I am positive and confident.

My unique contributions make a difference to others.

I feel great! This is a terrific day to be alive.

I am generous. I enjoy sharing what I have and what I am with others.

My work is going great. I enjoy what I do.

My smiles help others feel good about themselves.

I respect my attitudes and emotions. I am responsive to how I feel.

Problems in my life are eventually resolved.

I am getting stronger in body, mind, and spirit.

I use my time well. I enjoy being productive.

No matter what the weather is outside, my thoughts are pleasant and sunny inside.

I am in the right place and this is the right time for what I want to do.

I make positive, constructive choices for myself and others.

I am on my way to better health every day.

I stay focused on where I am. As I enjoy the present, the future takes care of itself.

I give my best every day.

I get things done on time, and others appreciate it.

My dreams can come true!

I am determined, and that attitude eventually eliminates all obstacles that confront me.

A Tisket, a Tasket, a Very Loving Basket

The wonder of setting aside differences

Things are changing quickly these days, particularly in the business of medicine. Small local hospitals are getting swallowed up by major medical corporations. Doctors are opening their own clinics or private offices so they can practice their own way. The result is that, in some places, the greatest disease is not something that can be seen by any piece of equipment but detected only with the human heart.

When former colleagues become competitors, the gravest symptom is an uneasy feeling of separation. But in one small town, "life support" took on a new meaning when two competing health-care providers decided to join forces to help a former employee. Wonders happen when we set aside our differences.

DEL HADN'T WORKED IN OVER A YEAR. He had recovered from ten different surgeries over two decades, but the last one disabled him permanently. He had worked at a small-town hospital for more than twenty years as a maintenance man. But now he was forced off the job long before it was time for his retirement.

Del had many friends on the hospital staff, and they were worried about him. They all knew that being out of work for such a long time had to take a toll on his family's finances, even though his wife was still employed. They decided to host a benefit for him and set to work.

The buzz in the halls of the hospital quickly became a dull roar. The theme of the event was gift baskets, and the more unusual, the better. People could make their own or work together in groups. Whole departments took on the project together, each trying to produce a basket brimming not only with goodies, but with fun and love for their friend.

The baskets were to be sold in a silent auction at the local Elks club. A local insurance company offered to match the proceeds. All the money would go to Del and his wife; the expenses for the dinner would be covered by a free-will offering. It was the best everyone could do.

But there was still one problem: Although the hospital employees would undoubtedly be as generous as they could be, the organizers knew the event would be more financially successful for Del if the local doctors and their staffs were involved. Unfortunately, the largest group of clinic physicians had left the hospital a year earlier and were now considered competitors. Relationships were strained, and formerly close friends sometimes found it difficult to cooperate.

Ironically, Del's wife worked for the clinic. Ultimately, that was the only excuse the chair of the hospital's committee needed to contact the physicians, administrators, and staff there and ask them to get involved. When she did, something wonderful happened. They responded enthusiastically, saying they appreciated the gesture of being included and would do all they could to help.

Soon, Del's colleagues in the maintenance department were putting up posters for the event all over the hospital. The marketing department of the clinic did the same, and the baskets started to arrive. The surgery department of the clinic sent over an antique silver tea service and several types of tea in a tray-sized basket decorated with fine linen napkins. The employees of the clinic's medical records department created a "movie night" basket filled with hot chocolate, mugs, a variety of videos, and popcorn. The housekeeping department of the hospital created a LEGO™ basket with enough of the toys to build a small city. The nutrition department of the hospital had a laugh filling a basket with "forbidden fruits" like candy and nutritionally empty snack food. The people in three of the hospital's departments went in together to fill a basket with fresh produce and a well-loved vegetable soup recipe. The daughter of the hospital's public relations director created a basket for cleaning buffs, filled with everything needed to make a home dust- and spot-free. The guys in maintenance created a "basket" of sorts out of old junk, including the cover from a discarded fan and some nuts and bolts. Deep inside, they tucked a gift certificate to a local restaurant. There were dozens of baskets, each more colorful and clever than the next. If there was any competition, it was only in the originality of the offerings.

The event was a huge success, not just because thousands of dollars were raised for a good man who had given his best to his employer, but because for the first time since the clinic separated from the hospital, people forgot their differences and relaxed. Former colleagues, now competitors, munched on burgers and placed their silent auction bids. But more important, they talked. Like people, like friends. For one sweet night, they did not see their differences; they saw only the same caring that had drawn all of them to the business of healing in the first place. And that was wonderful.

"My wife and I were very thankful for everything everyone did for us," Del said later. "But the best part of the evening was seeing everyone sitting around talking normally, just like they used to. The timing was perfect, because it looked like everyone was happy to get together and just relax."

♡ *Love Light: One for All*

Although you may not practice medicine or have any relation to the field, you might have someone in your life you consider a competitor. Take a moment to think about what you have in common: people you both know, similar experiences, complementary philosophies or ethics, and so on.

See if you can think of a way in which you can work together for the greater good of another person or cause. Then pick up the phone and suggest the idea. Keep the conversation and the activity lighthearted and fun. People love being part of a vision that is larger and greater than themselves. Music, food, games, and laughter are wonderful connectors. Focus on your goal, not your differences. You'll both be bigger for it, and so will everyone else who joins you.

The world needs each and every one of us. There is enough for everyone if we want there to be. Try living as if you believe that. It's wonderful.

Love Is All Around

The wonder of hope and help

I am always delighted but never surprised at how good most people truly are. All we need is a reason that feels right to us, and we'll willingly offer what we can of ourselves, often without condition or restraint. People love to take action, particularly when there's any hope that their contributions will make a positive difference.

This is never more true than when someone is sick. Many years ago, my mother-in-law became gravely ill with a combination of emphysema and the flu. A talented team of physicians did all they could and then told us to gather the family and prepare for the worst, since every major organ in her body had shut down except her heart. People wanted to help, but as far as I could see, there was nothing anyone could do. As we kept our bedside vigil, however, several members of the clergy came to see us. They each said the same thing: "We have a group in our congregation that is praying for her."

Miraculously, she got well. The doctors were shocked, and so was I. The experience made me hungry to know more about prayer chains and the power of focused love. The more I learned, the more I was convinced that wonderful things can happen when prayer and medicine are used together.

JOHN WAS DYING. Or so his doctors said. Supposedly, the cancer that had started in his kidneys would end his life in less than six months. Usually gregarious, he sat quietly in a corner at our friend Loretta's birthday party, possibly wondering if he'd ever see another birthday of his own.

He was alone when I approached him. "What if you're the one-in-a-million?" I asked.

He looked at me quizzically. "What do you mean?"

"Well, you know," I said. "There's always someone who wins the lottery, and someone who beats a terminal diagnosis. What if it's you?"

He smiled but shook his head. "I don't think so."

But I knew John to be a forward thinker, someone who embraced new ideas and wasn't afraid to take a risk. So I told him what I knew about visualization and prayer and how there was a growing body of evidence that both could improve a patient's chances.

"If you want, we could try it," I said. "Couldn't hurt."

John said he'd think about it and got up to leave. Suddenly, one of the men called us all into the kitchen. We formed a huddle around John, and the man spoke a prayer straight from the heart for his friend's well-being. When he was done, everyone was in tears.

The next morning, my phone rang. It was Loretta's husband,

Ken. He told me that John was leaving for more cancer treatment out of state. "Before he left, though, he asked if you would pray for him," Ken said. My spirit stirred, and I was surprised by the next words out of my own mouth, as they were more wonderful than what I would normally say. "I have a better idea. Let's get the whole town praying for him."

So Ken called John and asked if it would be okay for me to write a prayer and share it with some people we knew. He said fine, go ahead. What John didn't remember was that most of my friends were in the media, since I had been a columnist for the local newspaper for ten years. So besides our immediate friends, I faxed the prayer I wrote to the newsrooms of the radio and TV stations and newspapers in town. That's when something wonderful happened.

The media picked up on the story, and by the time John and his wife, Diane, returned, their mailbox was filled with cards and notes from well-wishers. Prayer circles had started all over town and were going strong. John's secretary e-mailed and faxed the prayer I had written to everyone on his Rolodex, and a powerful prayer chain had started. Because John was an aviator and dean of an aerospace school, he had friends and contacts all over the world. Now, people who were strangers to one another came together for a common cause, and the response was heartwarming.

We asked people to pray at 10 A.M. and 10 P.M. every day, since the Bible says, "Whenever two or more of you gather in His name, there is love." A group in Paris told us they were meeting at 5 A.M. and 5 P.M. their time, which put them in line with us. Contacts in China and Australia did the same thing, saying, "If one of us hurts, we all hurt. We're with you." The prayer chain took on a life of its own, and it wasn't long before people of all religions and denominations jumped in on the action, personalizing the prayer according to their spiritual beliefs.

The prayer did not ask for a specific outcome—under the circumstances, it would have been impossible to know what to pray for anyway. Instead, we simply asked God to take our love and use it for the highest possible good of John and his family.

With a sea of love swirling about him, John dared to think farther into the future. He tried visualization. He and Diane fell asleep every night to a customized tape that had soft music and words describing their family enjoying a summer day at their lake cabin.

The prayers continued, and so did John's medical treatment. Everyone in John's "Love Network" was given regular updates, and the prayers were changed monthly, acknowledging with thanks John's steady improvement. After three months, new tumors stopped appearing. Six months after the prayer chain started, the old tumors started to shrink. By the ninth month, he and his family were back at the lake. At one year, he was disease-free and spent the next eighteen months that way. He and his family and friends cherished every minute and made the most of them.

When the flood came, John's cancer returned. There was no way to reconvene the people who made up the nucleus of the prayer chain since the disaster had scattered them to unknown destinations. Even with the finest medical care, John died six months later. But he had lived three extra years, living every minute to the fullest. He left a legacy of love no one will ever forget. And that's wonderful.

◎ *Love Light: Willing Hearts*

Everyone knows someone who hurts. It could be someone with a chronic condition like emphysema, cancer, or diabetes or someone who suffers intermittently with problems like migraines or asthma. Assuming they are already receiving good medical care (prayer should be used as a supplement, not a replacement for medical care), you might want to ask them if they'd like to add prayer energy to their existing protocols.

If you are religious and belong to a congregation, ask if there is a prayer circle you could join. If not, try starting one. If you do not affiliate with a house of worship but enjoy exercising your spirit this way, you can start your own prayer chain simply by faxing, e-mailing, or posting the same prayer to everyone you know who might want to help. Anecdotal evidence suggests that these chains are most powerful when everyone prays at the same time of day; but if that is not convenient, every effort helps some.

Below is the basic healing prayer we used to start the prayer chain for John. As you can see, it is written entirely in the positive. When you pray for yourself or others, remember to pray *for* what you want, not against disease and fear. Author Sophy Burnham (*A Book of Angels* and *Angel Letters*) says that anecdotal evidence from people who have had near-death experiences suggests that when we pray something like "Please don't let John die!" all that comes through is spiritual static. God can create or destroy, but God can't *not* create. What is it that you are asking God to do? The spiritual picture you offered is still one of sickness and death, as "not" is a state of non-doing. Instead, create your prayer around what your heart truly wants: "Thank you, God, for helping John to live!"

If you'd rather not do the praying yourself, you can call Silent Unity, the largest and oldest Christian prayer chain in the world. They will pray with and for you, regardless of your denomination. There is no fee, and donations are optional. The number is toll-free: 1-800-669-7729. The National Center for Jewish Healing is in New York and offers booklets and liturgy for healing. They welcome inquiries at 212-772-6601.

Prayer may or may not contribute to medical cures, but one thing is absolutely certain: It plays a part in healing the hearts and minds of those involved. And that's wonderful.

A Prayer of Comfort and Healing
Source of Life,
We join together in love to ask Your help.
Be with us as our prayers go to _____.
May he/she enjoy a swift and complete recovery.
Let whatever healing treatments he/she seeks
Work comfortably and effectively.
We ask that only good come from the protocols he/she receives.
Add to that the love and good intention we offer now
And use it all for his/her highest good.
Lord, accept our prayer that pain and suffering, fear and doubt
Be relieved in all ways and Always.
Bless _____ and his/her family with love and life.
Strengthen each body; fortify each soul.
Open every heart to the wondrous bounty You have given us to enjoy.
Hold us now as we hold one another:
In faith and trust.
Bless us all with Your nearness and peace.
Thank You.
Amen.

The End of Anger

The wonder of self-acceptance

One of the greatest obstacles to wonder is anger. Anger not only leaves destruction of minds, bodies, and spirits in its wake, but it arouses fear, which blinds us to love's presence. Sometimes we can see anger. Other times, it is invisible to everyone but the person experiencing it. Sometimes, we can pick up on its vibrations just by entering a room. It may be silent, but there is what we call "an eerie stillness." That's anger, waiting to strike.

Anger is a difficult thing to release. Once it grips us, it holds on for dear life, demanding that we pay attention. If we try to ignore it, it will simply scream louder inside us until we take action. If we try to release it peacefully, it will give us reasons to hold a grudge. If we go into therapy to eradicate it once and for all, it can make the work painful and slow. It takes a lot of determination to end anger. But when we do, wonderful things can happen.

JIM WAS ANGRY. Anger was all he had ever known. Growing up, "one of the things I learned was that whoever yells loudest and longest wins." The third of four children, Jim learned to mask his anger with comedy. "We laughed a lot in our family, but it was always at someone's expense. Love was not expressed. For my parents, it was 'if you're eating, you've been loved.' So I became the family comedian to get attention."

At age thirty, Jim became a chiropractor, a decision he made after his father, also a chiropractor, came to an army hospital and adjusted Jim to enhance his son's comfort after a heart attack. "When he did that, my angina pains stopped instantly," Jim said. "That's when I knew I wanted to help people get out of pain."

When Jim opened his chiropractic practice, he did not think of himself as an angry person. "I had built up a pain threshold against anger, so I didn't even realize I had it," he says. "So here I am, going through my life basically thinking I'm a loving, caring person." In the office, he was. But with his family, Jim admits, "I was rough."

Jim had married, and he and his wife had three sons. Although he never expressed his anger with physical violence toward any of them, he found that he and his wife were constantly engaged in verbal battles that seemed to be escalating day by day. Finally, "I found I was getting angry for no reason," he says. "I couldn't tolerate the situation with my wife. I knew I had to get control."

Jim moved out, although he made a point of seeing his sons regularly. That's when he began a vigorous search for personal peace. Unfortunately, he was in a terrible car accident that ruptured two disks in his neck and one in his lower back. His new injuries aggravated a long-standing lower back condition, which forced Jim to stop his chiropractic work. He resigned himself to the change, knowing that if he was going to heal others, he had to heal himself first, in mind, body, and spirit.

During his physical recuperation, Jim took a job as a marshal on a local golf course. It was undemanding work that left him ten to twelve hours a day for reading.

"I met a lady on the golf course. To me, she was an angel," he says. "She introduced me to New Age books, including Marianne Williamson's *Return to Love* and *The Course in Miracles*. Jim studied the course faithfully and thoroughly. And then one day, another wonderful thing happened. As he was reading, Jim was overcome with a feeling of bliss.

"The room became totally light," he says. "I stood up, and it was like I weighed absolutely nothing. I laid back down and thought, 'I don't want to move. I want to be here.' "

The feeling didn't last long, but it was enough to inspire Jim to continue his vigorous, uninterrupted search for mental and spiritual well-being. He then met the director of the American Living Foods Institute and moved to the institute's grounds as its health-care director. There, he began reading works by Gourdjeff and Ospensky, authors who advocated integrating all parts of the self through communal living.

The residents of the institute met on a weekly basis to discuss subjects such as releasing judgments and learning what triggers anger in yourself and others. "The institute is where I made my biggest leap in handling my anger," Jim says. "I learned how anger physically felt in my gut, a tightening that worked its way up towards my diaphragm. When I became sensitive to that, I then had a choice. I could choose either to be angry or not to be angry."

One of the things Jim learned to do was meditate. "I uncovered in meditation that I felt I was not deserving of love," he admits. Then one day during meditation, Jim heard the phrase, "I deserve love because I am."

Jim meditated on that phrase for four months, day and night. He had another experience of bliss and knew finally, he says, that he was deserving of love. "The phrase 'I deserve love because I am' became a part of me, and I truly believed it," Jim says. "That's when I knew I could make the changes in myself that I wanted to make."

Within a month, Jim left the institute. He and his wife ended up in an amicable divorce. He continued to see his sons every weekend, and they grew closer. "The thing I was most thankful for was that I was able to become friends with my sons," he says. "My eldest son had picked up on some of my angry tendencies, but now he's working on realizing he creates everything in his life."

Jim now spends his days helping others eliminate anger. He teaches forgiveness workshops and is also a regional manager for Income Builders International, an organization that is attempting to change the model of the free-enterprise system from competition to cooperation. He's writing a book about his experiences, too. "I'm fulfilling my dreams," he says, "and I'm peaceful."

♥ *Love Light: Understanding Anger*

As Jim discovered, all of our emotions are played out first in our bodies before they go forth into the world around us. He knew when his anger was rearing its ugly head because he could feel it in his gut. You, undoubtedly, have a set of physical symptoms that are linked to your anger, too. Your head may pound, your palms may get sweaty, or your heartbeat may take off like a rocket. You might find that your joints stiffen or your face turns beet red. The next time you get angry, pay attention, and your body will give you the clues you need to manage your anger.

Start paying attention to your body's signals. You will quickly understand its form of communication, which will clearly tell you when you are thinking, saying, or doing anything that is bringing more suffering than happiness into your life. Once you can identify these, you will need tools to change what you do not like. You can try affirmations, honest and open discussion, meditation or prayer, taking a walk, or pounding a punching bag.

If you find that simple methods don't help you get a grip on anger, you may wish to seek professional counseling or go on a spiritual quest, as Jim did. You may need medication to help you get your anger under control. Whatever your budget or time constraints, there are programs available to help you.

When it comes to wonder, however, there is another way to look at anger. Sometimes anger hides the very thing we need to be happy, successful, or free. So if you find yourself constantly angry for the same reason, look closer before you try to silence the cue. Ask yourself, "What is the opposite of this?" In the answer to that question may lie the beginning of something wonderful.

Purple Ribbons

The wonder of helping someone you love

*E*veryone has a dream and the insecurity of wondering whether or not they're worthy of it. Very few of us take rejection well, so we avoid situations in which other people have the power to say no to us. We can refuse to put ourselves "out there," but then we suffer the ache of unrealized possibility. How would we feel if others wrapped their minds around our creations and took them to their own hearts? Even when we're willing to take the first step, sometimes it takes an intermediate step before something wonderful happens.

That step may not be ours to take. Instead, it might come from someone you love who sees things differently than you do. Often, we will resist these "intrusions," insisting that the success we seek come from our own—and only our own—efforts. But inside each of us is a loving soul that wants others to see the good in us, to make our best work visible to the world without hesitation or doubt. Wonderful things happen this way.

MY HUSBAND'S COFFEE was growing cold as he sat hunched over the breakfast table, poring over a small booklet like it was a number one best-selling novel. I peeked over his shoulder. "What 'cha doing?"

Steve kept a pen in one hand and his eyes on the paper as he spoke. "I'm entering some of my pictures in the county fair."

"Really!" I said, pulling out a chair for myself and sitting down. "I thought that they only gave out ribbons for prize petunias and cows and such."

He shook his head. "There's a whole collection of awards for arts and crafts, including photography. I think I'm finally ready to enter."

Steve's love of photography had grown steadily in our years together. What started as a casual hobby became a passion. Steve was snapping everything from flowers in our garden to huge landscapes to total strangers. He loved what he was doing and was practically gleeful each time he would return from the developer with the finished prints. He would spread these out across our kitchen counter, saying nothing but obviously hoping that the girls and I would *oooh!* and *ahhhh!!* over them.

But he never placed his beloved pictures under the scrutiny of a total stranger, much less an entire committee of them. He spent days trying to select exactly the right pictures to enter. He framed each one carefully, lovingly. He set them out not so much for our approval but his own, examining every centimeter to make sure they were perfect. Although every one Steve had picked out was technically excellent, none were the ones I knew sung to his heart or mine.

I said nothing when I accompanied him and our younger daughter to the fair pavilion, where he entered in the adult category and she in the junior one. After we handed in his and Erica's pictures, we browsed the displays. There were dozens of pictures, all of them beautiful in some way. As I gazed at them, I could feel the love the shooters had for their subjects. Suddenly, I knew what I had to do.

When we got home, Steve went back to work and Erica went up to her room. After they'd both disappeared, I went into our family room and stood before a framed 8"x10" photograph that had a place of honor in the middle of the largest wall. It was of a Scottish bagpiper, a man Steve and I had seen playing his instrument by the side of a rural highway on our first trip to Scotland. He wore a kilt made of one of the authentic tartans of the highlands and played his instrument with such sweetness that we could not resist pulling over and listening. He seemed happy to know that his playing appealed to us; and when we left, Steve took a picture of him. The result was an image that was not only technically excellent but filled with awe, both for the musician and the moment.

I took down the picture, even though doing so left an enormous hole in the décor of the most-used room in the house. But trusting that Steve had his mind on other things, I figured he wouldn't notice. I tucked the picture surreptitiously under my arm, called upstairs to my daughter to tell her I had to run an errand, and left.

I drove back to the fairgrounds and said to the woman at the registration table, "This is my favorite of all my husband's pictures. He forgot to enter it, so I will." She paused in her writing to gaze at it. "It is lovely," she said, smiling. As I turned to go back to my car, a sweet feeling of complete peace washed over me. For once in my life, I had an absolute sense that all was well.

Steve did not notice the missing picture, and I didn't mention it, since I didn't want to disturb his careful plan. He was up bright and early the next morning to head out to the fairgrounds to see if he or Erica had won anything; and I went along, humming softly as we rode along the highway. When we arrived, the woman at the front desk winked at me. "In the back," she whispered.

Steve had already found his way to the photography exhibit, but some of his pictures were missing. "They're gone!" he said in an anguished voice. "Do you think they were stolen?"

"The woman up front said to check in the back," I said calmly. "Maybe there were too many entries and they had to set up a different display."

We made our way to the back of the pavilion. As we approached, something wonderful happened.

The rest of Steve's pictures were there, all right. They were wearing blue ribbons—the mark of a first-place winner. The picture of the bagpiper also had a blue first-place ribbon on it. But that wasn't all. It was also wearing an enormous purple one, the award to the Grand Champion. It was the prize of all prizes, the one reserved for the item the judges believed to be the best in not just one but *all* the categories of the photography division.

At first, Steve was speechless. He just stood there grinning from ear to ear. But then he turned to me. "But I didn't enter this one!" he said.

"No, I did," I said. "When you weren't looking. You were so worried, you didn't even notice it missing from the family room wall."

He raised an eyebrow. "But why?"

I smiled. "Because it's wonderful. It's a picture you took with your heart."

❀ *Love Light: Little Deals*

It often takes less time and effort to help our loved ones than we think. I took Steve's picture from the wall, drove to the fairgrounds, entered it, and returned in under thirty minutes. You can even do it for total strangers. I was in the post office when the woman at the next station started to cry. She had a box that was half the size of a refrigerator, and when the clerk told her it was too big to mail, she started sobbing about how it was filled with five wedding dresses and needed to be in Las Vegas the next morning. He told her about a shipping service in town, but that only made her cry harder, since she said she was new to town and didn't know her way around. I walked over and offered to lead her there, and less than five minutes later, she had a big grin on her face as we delivered the box to people who could get it where she needed it to go. She got what she wanted and, for the price of a very few minutes, so did I.

Lots of people would call this "no big deal," but I like the term "little deals" better. If you are open to them, there are lots of "little deal" opportunities in your life every day. Just by doing one little deal, you can take away a source of tension or encourage a dream for someone else. To attract a few into your life, simply say, "I'd love to do a couple of little deals today that are easy and fun." Life will know exactly what you mean, and the service you find yourself doing will make you and someone else feel wonderful.

Little deals can make life's larger problems seem like no big deal. They can transform something that is seemingly insignificant into something very wonderful. They can make you feel confident, valuable, and free. Try doing a few, and you'll see for yourself.

A Tiny Miracle

The wonder of new life

*M*edically, we live in an exciting time. This is especially so in the case of premature infants. It wasn't so long ago that these tiny babies could not survive, let alone grow and thrive. But things have changed, and there are countless families who have been blessed by these little wonders. That said, life with a premature infant can be challenging. Nothing is certain, including survival. For all the joy a preemie brings, there is an even greater amount of anxiety shared by the parents, family, and friends. People don't know what to think, say, or do when a baby's life and health are at risk. When someone believes the best, however, wonderful things happen.

ONE POUND, SEVEN OUNCES. Megan Marie was no heavier than a loaf of bread and no longer than a ruler when she came into the world three months early. One week later, after she survived the first of three surgeries, her proud parents dubbed her "Mighty Megan."

"We never really thought she was going to die," her mother, Lisa, said. "When I was pregnant, she kicked so much that I knew she was one tough little girl."

That toughness was put to the test over a five-month hospital stay. Megan struggled with lung, digestive, and heart problems but made it through every ordeal. Through it all, Lisa and her husband, Bart, hung on with grit, love, and prayer, clinging to the hope that their tiny daughter would be okay.

In spite of their worries, Lisa and Bart sought no outside help other than prayer networks. "We just crawled into our shells and dealt with each situation," Bart says stoically. "We didn't want any kind of a support group," Lisa adds. Bart agrees. "None of the parents (of preemies) had the time or desire to talk to one another. We were all exhausted."

Family and friends stopped by, but their well-intentioned visits ended up heightening, rather than lessening, Bart and Lisa's fears. "People would look at Megan and say things like, 'I'm sorry.' Can you imagine? Here we have this beautiful little baby girl, and they acted like it was some kind of tragedy. We wanted to be congratulated, not pitied."

Then one day, something wonderful happened. A stranger dropped off a tiny burp cloth and bib for Megan. With the gift was the business card of a woman who made extra-small outfits just for premature babies. Lisa kept the card. Then, on what she calls "a particularly bad day," she went in search of the woman. She found her and her shop and immediately bought Megan three outfits — her daughter's first clothes. They were made of super-soft, colorfully patterned cotton knit, sewn together in a clever way so that Megan's medical equipment could pass through. "Putting an outfit on Megan made my day," Lisa says. "Suddenly we were looking at our daughter, not just at her wires and tubes."

After realizing how much this one simple gesture of congratulation had meant, Lisa and Bart hit on a plan. No doubt other parents of preemies would love to receive something similar, proof that their child was more than a patient with a chronic condition. So they formed "Minnie Miracles," a nonprofit organization that provides gift packs to the parents of premature infants.

They contacted area businesses, and donations started to arrive. A local department store gave $1,000 worth of assorted gifts from their baby department, including piggy banks and congratulatory cards. Lisa became friends with the woman who sewed the preemie outfits and made an arrangement to buy outfits for the gift packs at the wholesale cost rather than at retail. Lisa then called her local newspaper. They printed a story on the effort, and cash donations from well-wishers started to trickle in. Before long, Bart and Lisa had enough money to create fifty gift packs for parents at two area hospitals. Inside each gift pack were items that babies and parents of newborns love: Beanie Babies, receiving blankets, picture frames, and more, including the all-important preemie outfit, which was often the first item of clothing for each teeny-tiny infant.

Four years later, Megan is a healthy, active child who instantly delights visitors with her quick smile and gentle ways. Her growth has come slowly but in quantum leaps. "Once she started doing something like crawling or walking, she never went backwards," Lisa says. "It wasn't like she'd do it sometimes and not others." She smiles. "She just goes!"

Bart and Lisa have a folder full of thank-you letters for the more than 200 gift packs they have delivered since the Minnie

Miracles project began. They rarely meet any of the parents they serve but know they are making a positive difference. "We want to give hope to other parents of premature babies," Lisa says. "We know what we went through. Sometimes people would make mean comments like, 'Is your baby going to be normal?' or 'She's so tiny—don't you feed her?' " She looks over at her daughter, who is playing in the living room, and smiles. "We want them to feel happy and proud."

♥ *Love Light: The Gift of Sensitivity*

Although Bart and Lisa are sure their gift packs bring a smile to the faces of those who receive them, they both say the best gift is knowing what to say—or not to say—when a premature baby arrives.

Instead of "I'm sorry," say, "Congratulations!"

Instead of "I know exactly what you are going through," say nothing, unless you have a premature infant of your own. Let the parents tell you what is happening.

Instead of "Is your baby going to be normal?" try, "It looks like he/she is receiving the best possible medical care."

If the situation renders you utterly speechless, say so. It's okay to be shocked by what you see in a neonatal unit. Ask questions, but keep them objective. Try to keep your fears to yourself. Remember: Even tiny, fragile lives are worth celebrating.

If you want to do something wonderful in your town, consider starting a gift basket effort at your local hospital for the parents of premature babies. Or as described in "Love Is All Around," join a prayer chain and pray for each baby's strength and health.

Opening Minds

The wonder of bringing books to foreign children

*A*mericans tend to take books for granted. Not only are they readily available in schools and public libraries, but we can easily buy them everywhere we go: in the supermarket, the malls, even in gas stations. Our children are encouraged to read, and most do so eagerly. But that isn't true in some foreign countries. Books are in limited supply or are not available at all.

One of the paths to wonder is to do the thing we think we cannot do. This is especially true when we do something not only for ourselves, but for others. Challenges make us see wonders more clearly. They rise up in front of us like beacons of light on a far mountain. Although there is rarely a clear path that will take us to them, once they are found in our souls, it is only a matter of time and effort until we reach them in real life. Once achieved, no other wonders taste quite as sweet.

"WHEN I WAS A CHILD, I didn't know there was a larger world than my small town," Yohannes, an Ethiopian immigrant, says. "We had books in class, but our school did not have a library. The only libraries in Ethiopia are in big cities. And where I lived, there were no bookstores or books sold in the marketplace."

Yohannes's father died when the boy was only in third grade, and his mother didn't know how to read. But that did not stop him from developing a keen love of books. "In fourth grade, we read *Aladdin and the Wonderful Lamp*. By sixth grade, I was reading about the history of the Western world, Mesopotamia, and Ancient Egypt. Then we started with fiction. The stories fascinated me, and I would read my favorite books over and over."

Yohannes's world expanded in high school, when he was sent to a school 700 kilometers (about 435 miles) from his hometown. It was the early 1960s, a time when many Peace Corps volunteers were helping teach in foreign schools. Those who led Yohannes's classes introduced him to American literature, including *Rip Van Winkle* and *The Legend of Sleepy Hollow*. By the time Yohannes was in ninth grade, he was writing as well as reading stories. "I was fascinated by literature in general," he says. "I loved its beauty and how we can relate to it."

Although the high school had a library, it was purely for reference. Books were not checked out; and even though he was living in a larger city, Yohannes could find no bookstore. Then, due to a family problem, he was forced to drop out of school in tenth grade. He joined the navy, lured by its promise that it would help him "see the world." He never got very far from home, but he used his time in the military to read dozens of books from the navy library.

After two years, Yohannes decided that military life was not for him. He chose to finish high school in Ethiopia's capital city,

Addis Ababa. It was a good place for a young man who had now become an avid reader. Although books were expensive, they were available in local stores. Also, one of Yohannes's teachers encouraged him to borrow books from her private collection, which he was more than eager to do.

After high school, Yohannes's views of himself and the world around him continued to expand, and he was drawn to a political organization that opposed the government. It wasn't long before political pressure forced him to escape over the Sudan border, where he stayed for eight months until he was able to emigrate to Texas, where he had a friend.

He started a double major in journalism and anthropology at the University of Houston, transferred to the University of New York at Buffalo, and finished college with a degree in English literature. He traveled back to the University of Texas to get his master's degree in library and information science. A wonderful thing had happened: The boy who had no books was now a grown man working as a reference librarian.

Still, Yohannes was not satisfied. Although he could both read and speak English very well, he knew that most Ethiopians would never learn the language. And because of that, they would have very little to read. So after his college graduation, he formed African Sun Publishing, a company dedicated to producing books about Africa or in Amharic, the Ethiopian language. He published three: *The History of the Galla* (about the Oromo people of Ethiopia); *Yetint Mastawesha*, a book of essays, poetry, and letters written at the end of the nineteenth century; and *ABGD: Ethiopian Alphabet—Amharic English for Beginners*. He distributed his books in the United States, Canada, and Europe only, since he did not know where or how to place them in Ethiopia.

He eventually moved to Oakland, California, and became the children's librarian at the San Francisco Public Library. Once there, wonderful things started happening.

"I could see all these beautiful books that children enjoyed reading," he says. "I know that books can change lives. They can change societies. If I could get literature to the children of Ethiopia, I knew it would be a very, very important contribution."

So Yohannes started collecting books. He kept those he reviewed for *School Library Journal* and asked other librarians to give him their review books. He bought other books with his own money. "Day by day, week by week, whatever I'd get, I'd keep," he says. Within three years, he founded a legal nonprofit organization: Ethiopian Books for Children and Educational Foundation. The organization's mission was to establish a center for family literacy in Ethiopia where people of all ages could come and both read books and have books read to them in all languages.

Now, five years later, the foundation has 4,000 books. Unfortunately, the foundation has no place to put them in Ethiopia. "We know we want the first center to be in Addis Ababa," Yohannes says, "and expand from there." But the group needs money to build or secure a building and a lot of patience. Yohannes traveled to Ethiopia last year to make inquiries but ran up against a lot of bureaucratic hurdles.

He returned to the United States more determined than ever. "My dream is to make books available to children so they can read in their own language," he says. "And I hope to have families reading together, because I believe that families who read together are strong families."

He is sure that his wonderful vision will be fulfilled soon.

Love Light: The Wonder of Reading

Have you ever wanted to create something wonderful by making a difference? Reading is a great way to do it. If you really want to open a child's mind, read to him or her. If you don't have a child in your house, volunteer to read during story time at the library or in the pediatric ward of a local hospital. If you prefer the company of adults, you can join the many volunteers who take great pleasure in reading to the elderly in nursing homes.

If you're not a great reader but love the world of ideas, ask someone to read to you. It's an incredibly soothing activity to sit quietly with another person and let their voice lift the fog of a busy, distracted life. You not only will learn more than you knew before, but will surely feel closer and more connected to the person who is reading to you. Those are wonderful things, too.

If you'd like to help make something wonderful happen for the children and families in Ethiopia, you can contribute to Yohannes's dream by sending your check or money order to:

Ethiopian Books for Children and Educational Foundation
P.O. Box 21365
Oakland, CA 94620
(all contributions are tax-deductible)

The $100 Miracle

The wonder of little things that truly count

My father is like a gigantic umbrella: He's always there to protect his brood through life's stormy seasons. Other husbands and fathers do this, too, sometimes forcefully, sometimes quietly. And sometimes they do it even after they die. Not just through wills or estates, but with the sweet bonds of love. Even if our fathers aren't in the room, they can still make wonderful things happen.

JoEllen's dad had a secret. Hidden deep in the recesses of the old wallet he refused to throw away was a $100 bill. Supposedly, it was his "fun" money, although he never used it for himself. All four of his daughters knew he had it. Sometimes when he wasn't looking, little JoEllen would try to see if she could find his treasure, but she was never successful. The wallet was too complicated, or her father was too clever. But neverthe-less, there was not a single moment when she doubted the exis-tence of her father's $100 stash.

He once gave it to her as she was about to leave for a trip to Arizona. Although she was a grown, married woman with three children, her father knew that her spending habits could outpace her cash flow. So he gave her his legendary $100 bill "just in case." Proudly, she returned it to him when she came home one week later, and it disappeared into his wallet once more.

It would only be a few months before she would see it again. On April 19, 1997, as a massive flood forced the evacuation of their town, JoEllen and her family were set to flee. It was clear that she, her sisters, their mother, and father were going to have to split up and find shelter in different places. Her father brought his little clan together and reminded his sons-in-law to take good care of his girls and their children. Then he asked, "Does everyone have enough cash to last for a while?"

JoEllen naively replied that certainly she had cash—all of $15! While she expected to be home in a day or two, her father knew better. He reached in his wallet and handed her the $100 bill. This time, she was unable to repay it, "and even if I had tried, he never would have accepted it," she says with a tear and a smile.

The flood receded, months passed, and no one mentioned the $100 bill. When the family gathered for Thanksgiving, JoEllen's dad noticed a pair of 14-karat gold earrings in an advertising cir-cular. He decided he would buy them for his wife for Christmas. JoEllen and her sister Jinell agreed to do the shopping for him. But tragically, just three days later, he died from a massive heart attack.

As JoEllen and her family moved about in total shock and despair, she and Jinell came upon their father's wallet, which he had left, as always, on his bureau. JoEllen picked it up, remembering that he had given her the $100 bill during the flood and wondering if he had replaced it. As she slowly unfolded the corner flap, something wonderful happened. She saw that a crisp $100 bill had been neatly tucked into place. Neither sister said a word, but it was clear what they had to do.

The family was dreading their first Christmas without their dad. But on the morning of December 25, something wonderful happened for all of them. Tucked under the tree was a beautifully wrapped jewelry box for their mother. It had a tag attached with the same wording her beloved husband always used during their thirty-nine years of marriage. She wept as she read: "To Jeanne. Love, Santa."

♥ *Love Light: Fun Money*

Decades ago, when I was leaving home for college, my father gave me a $50 bill. He told me to fold it up and put it in my wallet "just in case." Years have passed and I have transferred that bill from wallet to wallet. Fortunately, I have never needed to spend it to get myself out of trouble. I have considered wasting it on something frivolous, but there has never been anything I wanted to buy that meant more than what the bill represents. It has actually increased in value to me over the years because it reminds me of something more precious than money—my father's love and his desire to protect me.

So just for today, put some cash in your wallet that you don't need right now. If you don't think you'll ever need it, give it to someone you love. If money is tight, make it $1 or even a fifty-cent piece. If you can, make it $10, $20, $50, or even $100.

Then forget about it. Months or even years may pass before

you or they remember it is there. But one day you may find that it's exactly the amount you need to make something wonderful happen either for yourself or someone important to you. When that occurs, do not hesitate. Wherever love is spent, it is just as quickly restored.

An Unexpected Compass

The wonder of finding your way

*M*ost of us prefer to avoid homeless people if at all possible. We look away when we pass them on the street. We'll offer $25 to a local shelter before we'll hand a single dollar to someone reaching up to us from a sewer grate. Homeless people remind us of loss — the most uncomfortable, challenging kind. Because we associate homelessness with poverty, we assume that the person who suffers from it is impoverished in all ways, not just by a lack of money.

But there are surprises. You never know what kind of mind or spirit hides within a body huddled up on a sidewalk. Sometimes, it is more like yours or mine than we want to admit. When we see others differently, we experience the wonder of human connection.

I WAS LOST. "Get off at the corner near the bank and look in all directions," the editor told me. "But I have to warn you — people always have a hard time finding us. There's no street sign, no number on our door, and no sign in our window. Good luck."

So I stood on a street corner 2,000 miles from home, hoping that something would tip me off as to the location of the publisher I had agreed to meet in less than ten minutes. I studied every building that didn't appear to be a gas station or retail store. There were five or six to choose from. I watched and waited, thinking that before long someone with an armload of books would come stumbling out of one doorway or another, signaling that a publishing house lay within.

No such luck. I carried no cell phone and considered using a pay phone to ask someone from the office to come outside and claim me. But a gang of tough-looking kids was standing by the only phone in sight, so I stayed put. I asked a clerk in one of the nearby shops if he knew which building was the right one, but he didn't have a clue. I started looking around for someone on the street who looked approachable.

I crossed the street to a bank with an outdoor automated teller machine and approached a well-dressed woman about my age. Unfortunately, she, too, did not know the location of the office I sought. As I stood there wondering whom to approach next, something wonderful happened. I heard a voice.

"Are you lost, Sweetie?"

The soft, gentle tones came from behind me. I turned, smiling with relief.

"Yes, I am. I'm looking for . . . "

I stopped midsentence. No one was standing there. Just as I thought I might be going a little crazy with worry, the voice spoke again.

"Down here, Sweetie."

I looked down to see a heap of a woman curled up on a single concrete paving block. She was wrapped in layers of a dingy brown fabric. Her hair was matted to her scalp and mostly gray. Her hands were bent, with knuckles like marbles and transparent skin like centuries-old parchment. I couldn't see her feet, which were hiding somewhere under her balled-up body. She could have been forty or ninety. Either way, she had lived too hard for too long. Was this really someone who could help me find my way?

She flashed me a toothless grin, and I couldn't help but smile back. "What you're looking for is in that building right over there." She uncurled one of her fingers and pointed in the direction of a white stone building on the corner, with an unmarked side entrance.

I wondered: Could she be right? What would someone who obviously had not worked in years know about places of business? But as I stood there, I realized she must know a great deal. People were coming and going at a furious pace, lost in thought or con- versation, ducking into shops and offices. Only this one lone homeless woman sat still, watching and listening. If this was her "spot," as I imagined it might be, she had probably memorized the patterns of everyone she saw regularly.

"Um, thanks," I said tentatively but gratefully.

"No matter," she answered and turned her attention away from me and toward the people leaving the teller machine with their fistfuls of cash. No one noticed her, whether by choice or dis- traction. She didn't have a bucket, cup, or hat to collect money. In fact, I started to wonder if she cared about cash at all. She just seemed content to sit and watch the passing action, as if it was her duty or pleasure to do so. She didn't look at me expectantly, waiting for me to acknowledge her help with a token of apprecia- tion. She simply gave of herself and retreated.

I started to walk away, but my feet felt leaden, as if I had for- gotten something. I realized that just like all the others, I had not recognized this woman. At first, I did not see her at all. How was that possible, I asked myself now, since her appearance and demeanor were in such total contrast to the scene around her? Even though I was blind to her, she was completely tuned in to me. She had obviously watched and listened and decided to respond. I wondered if she worried about my reaction or possible rejection. In many ways, I had to admit that her actions made her a stronger, more courageous person than I.

Once she did speak, I was reluctant to start a conversation, as her poverty made me uncomfortable. Her appearance frightened me like a bee buzzing around my body: I didn't know whether to stand still to prevent a sting or run away. I was thankful that although I was clumsy, she was not.

She appeared to be in need, but she did not act needy at all. In the moments of our exchange, she was actually the richer of the two of us. She offered me her knowledge unconditionally. She didn't say, "I'll tell you where it is, but first you have to pay me." She didn't hold out her hand even after she had made a contribution to my peace of mind. She didn't ask for anything, including my rather pitiful thanks. If anything, I was the one who had been begging up to that point, not just for information, but for a sense of where I belonged. She knew her place; I was still searching for mine.

As I saw things differently, I acted differently. I stood up straighter and felt the softness of the bay air on my face. I heard a soft crinkle come from my pocket as I did so. I reached in and felt a stray bill.

"Thanks," I said in a much louder, surer voice. Suddenly, I hoped that some of the other people around me could hear what I was saying. "You helped me out." I handed her the dollar.

She smiled again and pocketed the money. "You're welcome."

"You found us!" the editor exclaimed when I walked into her office.

"Not really," I answered. "It was more like I was found. The homeless woman on the corner gave me directions."

She walked over to the window and looked down.

"I would never have found this place if it wasn't for her," I said. "No one else had a clue how to find you."

The editor nodded. "Sign of the times. Everyone's in their own little world. Did you give her anything?"

My face grew hot, even though I was sitting on the shady side of the room. Had I done right by my unexpected guide? "Um . . . a dollar." I was starting to think that it wasn't enough, that I should have reached into my wallet and produced a ten or a twenty. So what the editor said next surprised me.

"Then you're even. You each found a little bit of what you wanted in the other."

☼ *Love Light: Getting Even*

We are naturally wary of strangers from the time we are very young because our parents tell us we should be. Whenever we meet someone new, we judge them by their appearance, their voice, or their demeanor. It's like buying meat that is wrapped in cellophane. It may look good in the package, but until we unwrap, cook, and consume it, we don't know how it will make us feel.

This superficiality works well for most encounters, since it is impossible to have soul-stirring relationships with every person we meet. On the other hand, we have an equally strong instinct to have our relationships—however brief—be meaningful and satisfying. So what are we to do?

We can get even. Usually, "getting even" makes us think of retaliation for something bad someone has done to us. Instead, I'd like to offer a different view of it: righting the cosmic balance. When we come into the presence of a stranger, we are thrown off balance. Who has the power here? In our minds, we ask the unspoken question, "What do you want from me?" or "Will you like me?" We wonder if this other person will take something from us, even something as intangible as our peace of mind. Fear is triggered before love.

Depending on the other person's state of mind, we come away feeling either triumphant or trampled. If they look away while we are talking, we think, "Is my conversation worthless?" If their eyes swallow us whole, scanning every inch of our bodies, we wonder, "Is something showing?" or "What does he/she want?" If the other person listens attentively but offers little of himself or herself, we miss the blessing of receiving. In first encounters, the scales of life are often tipped, leaving one person wanting and the other too full for comfort.

So the next time you meet someone new, start by taking a deep breath. Put down your drink or your briefcase and simply be present for a moment. Listen and watch to see if the teeter-totter of conversation and/or action is balanced between you. Keep things soft and simple. Save the probing about jobs, partners, and opinions for when—or if—you get to know one another better. If you do this, you won't feel restless, like there's someone "better" for you to talk to. You won't leave the conversation wanting, either. Enough will simply be enough.

When two people achieve balance in a conversation, the door to wonder opens. It may not always walk in at that time, but it is not hindered, either.

Give Me Shelter

The wonder of unlimited hospitality

I love a good coincidence, for it is a sweet reminder that life is not as difficult as what we think it is. This is especially true when we face dangerous circumstances and don't know what to do or where to turn. Sometimes we have to be at our lowest and most vulnerable for wonders to occur, since the rest of the time we are too busy trying to control life for them to appear.

Usually, we think of coincidences as one-shot deals. They amuse more than sustain us. We rarely, if ever, think of them as spanning generations. But if we look at our place in the universe differently, we can clearly see that time is only what we think it is. Nothing is random, and no good deed goes unnoticed by the invisible forces that surround us. What we call a "coincidence" is the wonder that life reliably delivers what we need just when we need it the most.

WHEN THE GRADUATION INVITATION CAME, I looked at Steve. "Let's go," I said, "even though we don't know the family well."

We had met Clif, the graduate, only once, when he came to our home so we could interview him for our alma mater. He was a delightful young man, thoughtful and polite, with a strong desire to see the world and make the most of his life. We liked him immediately. When the interview was over, we stood up to say our farewells, not really expecting to see each other much, if at all, in the future.

But when Clif sent us an invitation to his high school graduation, we decided to go, figuring his family would likely be as pleasant and interesting as he. We were right. Marie, Clif Senior, young Clif, and their other son, Peter, extended a warm and hearty welcome to us, despite the fact that we were virtually strangers. Their farmhouse was the most unusual we'd ever seen. They'd built an aviary on the main floor, and the living room was covered with artifacts gleaned from their travels on many continents. They enchanted us with real-life adventures that mixed hometown common sense with worldly wisdom. Although the afternoon was perfect, when we left, we really didn't know if or when we would see each other again.

Many months later, the flood forced us to evacuate our home and our city. My husband and I decided to travel west, although the nearest hotel with an available room was more than 300 miles away. Plus, we had our dog and had no idea where we would put her for the month or more the mayor said we would have to be gone. "I'm going over to the office to pick up a few things," Steve said resolutely. "We'll just have to punt from there."

He wasn't in the office two minutes when something wonderful happened. The phone rang. "Steve? This is Marie," she said. "We heard about what's happening there. Do you need a place to stay?"

It took Steve a moment to realize to whom he was speaking, but once he did, he grinned from ear to ear. "Yes! Thank you!"

"And bring Lady," Marie said, referring to the collie she only knew from our description. "She's welcome, too."

Amazingly enough, their warm hospitality extended not only to the four of us and our dog, but to half a dozen other evacuees and their pets. Both their sons abandoned their bedrooms to make them available to us. Somehow, juggling various furniture and room uses, we all managed to fit comfortably. We grabbed folding chairs and any other seat we could find and made ourselves at home around their kitchen table for meals. For two days, their home was not only a safe haven; it was a place of spiritual renewal where we found both the relief and strength we desperately needed to make better plans for the challenges ahead. When we left, our dog stayed behind with them for well over a month until we could make our flood-damaged house habitable again.

Almost a year later, we invited their family to our house for dinner to thank them for their incredible hospitality. Steve's father, Sam, who had lived in the area for more than eighty years, joined us. Usually gregarious, Sam was uncharacteristically quiet throughout the meal.

Suddenly, he spoke up. Sam looked at the elder Clif quizzically. "Did your father have a limp?" he asked.

Clif looked surprised. "Why, yes. He did. He had polio as a child."

Sam smiled. "I remember him. He came to town when I was a boy, and he needed a place to stay. My parents had an empty room and took him in. And now you took in my son and his family. I guess what goes around comes around."

We all looked at one another and smiled.

Wonderful.

☺ *Love Light: What Goes Around*

The world is a much smaller place than any of us want to admit. It is said that a butterfly flapping its wings in Brazil can change the ocean currents off Florida. Whether you believe that or not, it's fun to think that when you perform an act of kindness for someone, ripples of energy carry it far beyond where it was first delivered.

Think about any time when you did something nice for someone else, particularly if you did so without any expectation of what you'd receive in return. Then think about the days, weeks, and years that followed. Can you see the reflection of what you did in something wonderful that happened to you? It's likely that you can.

Some people call this "The Law of Karma." In other words, what goes around, comes around. Metaphysicians say that it is impossible for us to hold a thought about another human being that is not reflected back to us in some way. Judge someone, and you will be judged. Help someone, and when you need it, you will be helped. Love unconditionally, and love will find its way to you.

This idea is summed up by the Golden Rule: "Do unto others as you would have them do unto you." Don't do it thinking that these people will specifically do this for you if you do that for them. Wonder doesn't work that way. It comes in treating every person you meet as God incarnate. You may help one person and get the favor returned by a total stranger. For example, I had given directions around our convoluted neighborhood streets to countless drivers before the homeless woman showed me the way to my appointment. And don't expect an immediate tit-for-tat payoff. It might take decades before you see the reflection of your kindness again. But sometimes, that's the most wonderful thing that can happen.

Someone Who Cares

The wonder of believing in someone

We've all heard judgments such as "He's a good boy" or "She's a bad student." It is all too easy for adults to label children and even easier for children to accept what we believe to be true about them. There have been studies in which a teacher is given a classroom full of academically challenged students but told they are gifted. The teacher's attitude and actions mirror that belief, and the students' test scores all rise. The opposite has also been proven true—if a teacher thinks he has a roomful of "dummies" on his hands, even if the children are actually gifted, test scores sink.

Sometimes we form our opinions based not on what one person believes, but what many believe. Again, this is especially true for students, who pass from teacher to teacher. One year's bad performance can become a career nightmare, where teacher after teacher expects the worst, even before the student walks in the door. It is impossible to underestimate the potentially destructive power of a group belief. It is a kind of psychic "ganging up" not just on the person who is the subject of the beliefs, but on all others who might dare to think of the student differently.

But wonders can and do happen. They take a strong-willed individual who says, "I'll decide for myself, thanks." When a teacher can ignore years of judgments and labels to reach a student, the lost can be found. One shift of perception, one person willing to rise above the challenge of negative opinions, can change many lives for the better.

ANTHONY'S TEACHERS HAD GIVEN UP HOPE. In the days before attention deficit disorder was diagnosed, Anthony couldn't sit still and wouldn't pay attention. As a result, he became labeled as stupid and unteachable. One of his high school teachers told him, "The only thing you're good for in life is stopping enemy bullets."

When Bobbi met Anthony, she had been warned to expect the worst. Indeed, things didn't look promising, at least not at first. Although he was fifteen, Anthony liked to eat chalk. He also liked to throw his highly sharpened pencil against the ceiling tiles to see if he could make it stick.

In spite of her colleagues' warnings and Anthony's off-putting behavior, Bobbi was undaunted. As the teacher in charge of the high school's resource room, her job was to assist students who had learning and other problems. "I see something good in all my students," she says confidently. "In a class of thirty kids, that's hard to do, but I only work with a few children at a time. I never give up on them—I tell them they're going to pass and that they can go to college if they want."

Anthony would be no different. Quickly, Bobbi became his number one guide and cheerleader. She helped him organize his homework. She patiently explained things he didn't understand. She reviewed material with him for all his tests. But mostly she kept saying, "You can do it, Anthony. You can do it."

Even with Bobbi's encouragement and guidance, Anthony struggled throughout his high school career. She went to see his teachers to get his assignments and then would work with him for ten or fifteen minutes every day until he could focus and understand the work that was his to do. Eventually, her persistence paid off. Anthony started finishing his assignments and felt a sense of accomplishment from keeping his mind on his work.

Bobbi worked with Anthony for three years. Throughout the entire time, Anthony's father was equally supportive, doing whatever he could to help his son stay on track. By seeing the good in him, something wonderful happened. The boy whom a decade of teachers had written off as a loser became a winner. He graduated from high school. When Anthony graduated, his father was so proud that he bought him a truck, which Anthony drove to his celebration dinner.

Anthony joined the Marines after high school, and Bobbi didn't hear from him for a while. Years passed. Then one day, another wonderful thing happened.

Bobbi was in the resource room when a tall, handsome young man walked in. The face was Anthony's, but the confidence and maturity in his stride were not those of the boy she knew. "You had faith in me," he said happily. "I wanted to come back and tell you that I did great in the Marines." He went on to tell her that he left the service and went to work for United Parcel Service, where he eventually became an assistant manager. When he left that job, he became a stockbroker.

Anthony sounded as though he was succeeding in his quest to make a life for himself. So what he said next surprised Bobbi.

"Now I want to go to college," he said. "Will you be my reference?"

Of course, Bobbi said yes and wrote an enthusiastic endorsement for Anthony. He chose a college with a strong program for learning-disabled students. But even with improved confidence, things were challenging for Anthony. He used a recorder to tape all of his classroom lectures. He forced himself to learn how to use a computer competently. He asked for extra time when he took his tests. Slowly but surely, he succeeded. And in December 1999, he graduated with honors and a 3.8 cumulative grade point average.

Then one more wonderful thing happened. Anthony decided to become a lawyer. He passed the LSATs (Law School Admission Tests) and was accepted to not just one, but three law schools. He chose one of the finest law schools in New York, not just because of its reputation, but because they were happy to offer him a huge scholarship.

Today, Anthony loves giving speeches and telling other people they can do it. He also tells them that he started to succeed when someone first believed in him. And that someone, he says, is Bobbi.

"Not every child is going to become an academic genius like Anthony," she says, "but if you believe in children, they will respond. It's just a matter of someone caring for them."

☉ *Love Light: You Get What You Expect*

I once heard a motivational speaker named Lee tell a hilarious but true story about a man who had a hair-trigger temper. His wife tried everything to stop his rages, but nothing worked. Finally, in desperation, she decided to try encouragement rather than resistance. When he blew his top, she said gently, "You know, dear, it's not like you to get upset about something small like that." Every time he would get angry, she would remind him of how reasonable and calm she wanted to believe he was. Finally, after six months of hearing this new belief, there came a day when the man started to lose his temper and then abruptly and without warning hauled himself up short and mumbled, "You know, it's not like me to get upset about little things!" He walked out of the room quietly.

We get what we expect from others. The trick is to learn to expect the best, especially from those who are "dis-eased" by doubt, anger, or despair. Like Bobbi, we need to form our own opinions and not allow our perceptions to be colored by other peoples' experiences, doubts, or fears. If we learn to say, "Well, that is what is true for you, but it may not be what is true for me in this case," we leave the door open to wonder.

Next, we must remember that we cannot change other people's lives. We can only remind them that it is possible for them to do it themselves. Bobbi did not do Anthony's work. She just helped him organize it. She also did not take his tests, write his papers, or go to work and do his job. He did all of that himself. She was his guide and cheerleader through the dark and twisted path to success, but Anthony still had to walk on his own. She merely held the flame aloft, steadfast and true.

Along that route, Bobbi played Show and Tell. She showed Anthony what he needed to do to succeed and told him over and over and over that he could do it. Eventually, we believe what we are told about ourselves. And even though dozens of people had told Anthony that he was a failure, all it took was just one person who believed in him—and said so—to spur him to success.

Finally, Bobbi had patience. The change in Anthony took years, not minutes. Anthony had built a life around who he believed he was, which was not something that was going to change quickly or easily. Before he could succeed, it was not just

Bobbi who had to see him differently. He had to change his own perspective about himself.

It's as easy as 1-2-3 to make a wonder like this appear in your own life: (1) Tell someone who is struggling, "You can do it!" Say it out loud, and say it often. Even if you don't fully believe it, keep saying it until you both get used to hearing it. (2) Show and tell the person who is struggling how to fix the problem that is holding him/her back. If you don't know how, find someone who does. Do not do the work for them, whether that be mental, physical, or spiritual. (3) Celebrate improvements along the way. For in journeys like this, there are many wonders, not just one or two. Enjoy the varied delights of uplifting another human life!

The Lawyer

The wonder of realizing you can do it

When we feel bad about ourselves, we often try to fix what we see in the mirror. Rarely do we dig deep into our own souls, where true radiance lies. In the previous story, you met Bobbi, sharing her wonder as her encouragement of her student Anthony paid off. Here is the other side of the story. Anthony explains that nothing wonderful can happen until you see it in yourself.

"I HAD ZERO CONFIDENCE IN MYSELF," Anthony says. "I believed I had nothing to look forward to. I barely passed high school and didn't think I'd ever get into college."

Nothing ever came easily to Anthony. His mother died on his first birthday. His dyslexia went undiagnosed, and he struggled to learn right from the start. He changed schools more than half a dozen times before he was in fifth grade. "I was always in trouble because I never did my homework right, stuff like that," Anthony says. "I used to get in fights because people would put me down and I would try to defend myself. I was always a nobody. After a while, I just accepted it. I made a joke of it—I pretended I was lazy. I acted tough, but it wasn't me."

Because of his work with Bobbi in high school, Anthony's self-esteem improved slightly. After graduation, he joined the Marines. "I chose the Marines because they're the best," he explains. "The Marine Corps has the reputation of being a tough place to succeed. I did really, really well in boot camp and graduated." Anthony then joined a Marine reserve unit in the Bronx. "I traveled a lot with the Marines, but I was home a lot, too. I needed a job, so I applied at UPS and got hired right away."

But once again, Anthony's hard-earned confidence started to slip away. In the reserves, he lost his "edge." He decided to try one college course but quickly flunked out. "I didn't have anybody helping me," he says. "I wasn't organized and didn't know which way to turn." Even though Anthony loved the history he was studying, "I had a really bad writing problem, and I was too self-conscious to write the final essay."

Anthony hoped to make a success of himself without a college degree. By the time he was nineteen, he was made a supervisor. But once again, his fear of limitation caught up with him. "When it came time for a big promotion, I didn't get it because I didn't have a college diploma," he says.

A friend told him he could make a lot of money as a stockbroker. "To me, that sounded so prestigious, so intellectual," Anthony says. "I wanted to try it." He got the required books, studied night and day for a month, and passed the exam on his first try. Soon, he was working twelve hours a day, six days a week, and making good money. But something deep inside him still nagged at him. He wanted to go to college.

The day he left the brokerage, Anthony drove directly to a college that Bobbi had told him about in high school, one that had an exceptional program for learning-disabled students. "I went right in, sat down, and gave them the sixty-dollar application fee," Anthony says. "Then I kept my fingers crossed." Bobbi, his former tutor and cheerleader, became his strongest reference. He was accepted and started classes a few weeks later.

Anthony was promised two tutors in the fall but, in his eagerness to get started, enrolled in a computer class over the summer. He worked harder than he ever had in his life, and then something wonderful happened.

He got his first A.

"It was the first A I'd ever gotten in my life," Anthony says jubilantly. "It was like a drug. If you've had A's your whole life, you're used to them, but when you're supposed to get an F and you get an A, it feels *so* good. I didn't want anything other than A's after that." Anthony signed up for a second computer course, and this time earned an A+. By fall, he was mentally and emotionally ready to take as many courses as the school would allow him. He didn't want to be in school "forever," since he was living off his savings as a stockbroker and some money that his mother had left to him and his sister.

Anthony worked hard and started getting A's regularly. Unaccustomed to success, "I still doubted myself," he admits. But after his third semester with a 3.7 grade average, he found himself thinking, "Well, maybe I'm onto something here."

Anthony continued this way through the spring and summer, until it came time for him to take a required math course. "I was scared," he says. "This was algebra, not simple addition and subtraction. I went for more tutoring, studied like I never did before in my life, and I got an A." He later took three other math classes and became so proficient that he started tutoring other students.

By the time Anthony was in his junior year, he was getting "fantastic" grades and had secured a position as vice president of the National Honor Society. His confidence had finally grown to the point where he felt he could start to dream about becoming a lawyer. He started studying books on history, politics, and the legal profession. Finally, he felt he was ready to take the LSAT. But then, "I bombed the practice test and figured I'd never get in." That began "the most miserable summer of my life," as he dedicated himself to studying twelve hours a day in the library. As he jogged at night, he visualized getting a high grade. He prayed.

But Anthony still had a problem: "I needed extra time for the test because I read slow and I don't write well." One of his teachers took up his cause, petitioning the testing board to make an exception for Anthony. They forced him to take an IQ test to prove that he needed the extra time, which was eventually granted. As a result, "I got a really good grade on the test—more than the goal I had set for myself," Anthony says proudly.

Anthony applied to three law schools. "I would run home every day and check the mail," he says. And then one day, another wonderful thing happened. "I came home and opened up the mail and it said, 'We are pleased to inform you that you have been accepted . . . ' " Anthony had gotten into the law school of his choice with a $27,000 scholarship.

Then he did one last wonderful thing. "I took the acceptance, put it in Saran Wrap, and laid it at my mother's headstone," he says quietly. "I gave a copy to my mom, and it's still there. I always feel that she's with me. I know for a fact that she's here, helping me out." Anthony's father is his helpmate here on earth. "He's my best supporter and my best friend," he says.

"Now I think I can be anything I want to be if I'm willing to sacrifice, put in the time, and do what needs to be done," Anthony says confidently. "A journey of a thousand miles must begin with a single step."

☙ *Love Light: Who Says So?*

Although Anthony had a learning problem, his sense of failure came largely from the negative comments of others. He came to believe what they said about him.

Fortunately, somewhere down deep, he knew that the "tough guy loser" they saw was not him. But even with encouragement and help, he did not feel like a winner until he had a string of successes both in and out of school. Today, he still struggles with self-doubt, although far, far less than before. And he speaks publicly to students of all ages, motivating them with his personal courage and perseverance.

So, quick! Ask yourself: What word pops into my mind when I describe myself? Once you have it, look closer: Whose word is it? Yours or someone else's? Where did you get it? When? Does it fit who you want to be?

If it does, celebrate! But if not, pick out a new word or phrase, one that you really, really love. Start using it in all areas of your life. Tell other people about it. Build your life on what you want to be true about you, and soon others will see it, too.

Now, doesn't that feel wonderful?

Heavenly Cash

The wonder of receiving unexpected money

*M*any, many people wish they had more money. Rather than work hard for it, they'd prefer that it fall out of the sky or turn up in some wonderfully unexpected manner. It often does, but not in an amount we consider "enough." We find a penny on the sidewalk or a couple of quarters in the coin return of a vending machine. We reach into the pocket of last year's winter coat and find some forgotten cash in the pocket, or we receive a bill for an amount far less than what we expected. Whatever the amount, I like to believe that it turns up to remind us that "little wishes" are being granted all the time. I call found cash "angel money," because it always feels like it's been heaven-sent. Sometimes the angels can be particularly generous. When your heart is in the right place, wonders happen.

EVERYONE KNOWS HARRIET as "The Angel Lady." Besides her love of angel art and lore, she is considered an "earth angel" by her many friends across the country. She is especially responsive to cancer patients, and if she hears of anyone who needs support, even a total stranger, Harriet is quick to send an angel gift to remind them of the invisible forces of love that are here to comfort and uplift us all. Cards, candlesnuffers, papier-mâché boxes, pens, books—Harriet's generosity stretches as far as her fixed income will allow. Even in the leanest times, she somehow manages to buy, package, and send angel gifts to others. She takes pride in knowing that her angel reminders are often just what people need to receive, just when they need it most.

One day, Harriet and her friend Juliette were discussing aging. "One of the negative aspects of getting older is the fear of running out of money after you've retired," Harriet said. At seventy-five, she was trying to conserve her precious savings, since the income from the interest and her social security were her only "pension." Sometimes, cancer patients would have to wait for their angel packages because the income from her savings was fully allotted at the moment.

As Juliette left that day, Harriet surprised her with this statement: "You know what? Somehow more money will come. I still enjoy sending angel packages. That won't stop."

One statement of faith was all it took. The next day, something wonderful happened.

Harriet went to the mailbox expecting to find little more than circulars and bills. But to her surprise, there was a personally addressed letter. Upon opening it, she discovered that a recently deceased uncle had left her $2,000. Harriet had always been fond of this uncle and his wife, and they of her, since they had no children of their own.

"Perhaps he heard me yesterday," she said later. "In any case, I believe in angels, and this money arrived so I could continue my angel work."

♥ *Love Light: Ask an Angel*

There are many ways for wishes to come true. One is when we go after them ourselves. When we face a challenge or defeat a fear, wishes often come true. Another way is for others to act as "earth angels" for us, opening doors and coming through at times when we are too weak or uncertain to do so ourselves. But my favorite way to have a wish come true is to ask an angel. I have experienced too many wonders in my own life not to believe in these invisible friends, and I call upon them regularly. They stand ready to help you, too, and not just in times of imminent danger. From what I've seen, they'd rather be our playmates than our heroes. Angels have gotten me great parking spaces in busy malls, produced friends I was longing to see, or delivered some sort of humorous message that snapped me out of a dark mood.

If you want something wonderful to happen, put the angels to work. Make a simple, playful request you believe could come true. Or better yet, follow Harriet's lead and make a statement of faith. Don't worry about how or when it will occur. Just believe in angels . . . and wonders.

A Hug from God

The wonder of divine reassurance

*I*n the Bible, Moses goes before Pharaoh to tell the ruler that God wants him to free the Hebrew slaves. Pharaoh refuses, mostly because he has no proof that God exists. So God produces the ten plagues, which eventually cause Pharaoh to change his mind and let the people go. From that moment on, wonders happen.

Today, hundreds of millions of people believe that God exists. But when trouble comes, we often look for signs of reassurance. "I need some proof that everything is going to be all right," we say, but often we are too weary with fear to look. It's hard to believe that God has not abandoned us.

This is especially true when a child gets hit with a terrible illness. Although it appears that God has left the room, it may be that the Source of Life has never been closer. Ironically, it is often when we or those we love are most vulnerable that a sign of God's nearness appears. When we look up from our misery, there it is.

ANDREA NOTICED A SMALL LUMP on her right arm, just above her wrist. At sixteen, she played varsity tennis and thought it might be a ganglionic cyst. Although it bothered her, she waited until tennis season was over to see her surgeon. He, too, thought it was a cyst and suggested that she leave it alone unless it began to hurt.

Just two weeks later, Andrea woke up abruptly one morning and said she wanted the cyst removed right away. "It's as though an angel came to her at night and said, 'Just do it,' " her mother, Madelyn, says.

Andrea had outpatient surgery. "The surgeon said it looked like a tumor," Madelyn remembers, "although at the time I thought it must be benign—I didn't think he looked concerned."

But she was wrong. The tumor had many different kinds of cells, which forced the pathologists to test and retest it. Eventually, they classified it as a liposarcoma, which surprised the doctors. Liposarcomas usually appear in the elderly, not in an otherwise healthy sixteen-year-old.

The family traveled to the Mayo Clinic, where doctors continued to test the tumor. In spite of its mixed content, it was a grade level 3, which meant the doctors wanted to treat it aggressively. With a six-inch incision, they did exploratory surgery on her arm, which fortunately showed only healthy tissue. Still, they implanted a radioactive seed and scheduled twenty-three additional radiation treatments as well as chemotherapy for a full year. Every three weeks, Andrea would have to be hospitalized, since the treatment put her at risk for dehydration.

Although at first Andrea only worried about dying, when she heard of the treatment, her response was, "I'd rather die than lose my hair." She was angry. But she also expressed a strong faith: "God won't give me anything I can't handle."

Her first chemo treatment was difficult. Andrea was still

groggy from the surgery that put a Portacath in her chest, and she threw up all night when the medicine was introduced. Finally, her doctors gave her a strong medication so she could rest. By that time, Madelyn and her husband were emotionally and physically spent.

"My husband wanted me to go back to the room and rest because I was so exhausted," Madelyn says. "I was too upset to sleep, but I went back to the hotel room, which was right across the street, to take a bath and freshen up." As she left the hospital, something made Madelyn stop and turn around. When she did, something wonderful happened.

"I looked up, and there, right next to Andrea's room, was a statue of Jesus that looked as if he was holding her room in his hands," she says. "It was as though God was saying, 'Madelyn, I have her in my arms. She's going to be okay.' I went back to my room and knelt down and prayed and prayed. When I was done, I just knew in my heart that she was going to be okay."

Madelyn took her bath and went back to Andrea's room. As she approached the door, she heard the glorious sound of her husband's laughter. "I walked in that room and Andrea was sitting up, eating a Popsicle and some Jell-O," she says gratefully. "And I thought, "Thank You, Lord. We're *all* going to be okay."

Love followed Andrea everywhere she went. After being away from home for three full months, the teen was afraid to return to school because she had lost her long hair, eyebrows, and eyelashes, as well as a lot of weight. She didn't want her friends and the other students to stare. But a wonderful high school counselor gathered the students together and prepared them, and Andrea was welcomed back to school with open arms. When she had to be hospitalized for her chemotherapy treatments, the hospital personnel gave her a private room away from others so her friends could come over and watch movies with her late at night. Her dad even popped popcorn for the gatherings and delivered it to them.

Andrea stayed on the cheerleading squad and kept up her figure skating. Sometimes her toes would get numb from the anti-cancer drugs, and she lost her balance easily. But she continued on and eventually became a skating coach.

"Her father, LeRoy, and I wanted to keep her in a bubble," Madelyn says. "But she wouldn't hear of it." Andrea had been working with her church's youth group to go to a gathering in Atlanta. Most of the kids were going on a bus, which would have been impossible in her condition. Andrea wanted to fly, but her parents would not allow her to fly alone while she was in treatment. Wonderfully, there were two Midwest organizers traveling by air to the event. As it turned out, there was just one seat left on their plane, which just happened to be right between the two of them!

Andrea's doctors gave their okay, provided they could give her a blood transfusion before she flew. That done, they made arrangements for her to get a checkup while she was in Atlanta at a clinic that turned out to be just a few blocks away from her hotel. "Faith and determination will get you a long way, " Madelyn laughs.

At Andrea's five-year checkup, her doctor said the words she had been longing to hear: "There's no reason why this cancer should return. It's done."

Andrea recently married the love of her life and began a career in elementary education.

Wonderful.

⑨ *Love Light: Give It Up*

Even on the darkest days, there is light around us. To find it, surrender. Usually, we have to be at our most frightened or vulnerable, which was certainly true in Madelyn's case. She received her sign when she was weary beyond belief, much too tired to demand anything of anyone, much less God.

The wonder-maker in this story is actually Madelyn's husband, who suggested she return to the hotel, rest, and freshen up. The best and easiest way to surrender is simply to leave the room. Give up on the situation, if only for a short while. Change your focus. Go somewhere else. When you shift your energy from negative to neutral, wonders often appear.

Finally, get wet if you can—showers, baths, whirlpool baths, and swimming pools are excellent cleansers of both body and spirit. Water is often used as a metaphor for emotions, and it is through water that we experience many of our life transitions, including birth, baptism, mikveh (ritual immersion pool used by Jewish women), and so on. We get clean in water. We float in water. Try letting it wash away your fears or hold you above life's burdens.

Although Madelyn took her shower after seeing the statue hugging her daughter's room, the water renewed and revived her in a much-needed physical way. But I know of other stories of people who took a thirty-minute bath with closed eyes, only to open them and see wonders soon after. Do what feels right to you.

Let go. God can't put anything in your hands if they're clenched in a fist.

Puppy Ciao

The wonder of healing touch

Of all the wonders in the world, few are more amazing than those involving healing of our physical bodies. This is not only because we dread illness, but because good health makes it far easier to get the most enjoyment from life.

These days, there are wonders being performed on and by our physical bodies as never before. Doctors and technologists are able to repair and create tissue in wonderful, seemingly miraculous ways. As allopathic medicine advances technologically, so do some of the complementary healing arts. We want to know our own ability to heal using not only good health practices, but with power supplied by our minds and spirits. Practices like meditation, biofeedback, massage, and visualization are moving into the mainstream, and more and more people are incorporating them into their recovery programs.

One of these growing practices involves Healing Touch,

which works with the energy vibrations around the patient's body. Our bodies are composed of atoms and molecules that are always in motion. We are, in essence, walking, talking energy machines driven by our hearts and souls. The energy we give off can actually be seen with a Kirlian camera. It looks like a halo of light that surrounds our entire body. Healing Touch Practitioners manipulate this "invisible" energy field to remove blockages and correct imbalances. The practice involves faith and trust both in oneself and in the loving force that fills each and every one of us. When this faith is rewarded, it is a true wonder.

JoAnn was baby-sitting her infant granddaughter. When a delivery man brought a parcel, JoAnn didn't notice that her son and daughter-in-law's black Labrador retriever had broken free of his chain and that their puppy, a golden Lab, had also disappeared. Although the older dog returned, the puppy did not. When JoAnn's son came home later that afternoon, they searched until it was time for supper. JoAnn had to attend to her mother and left reluctantly at that point. "I got a phone call about eight-thirty that they had found the dog in a trap," she says. "They had heard his whimpering and followed the sound. But that also meant that his little paw had been crushed for about eight hours."

JoAnn's son and daughter-in-law were doing all they could to ease the puppy's pain and asked her to please come over and do a Healing Touch session on the injured paw. When JoAnn left nursing to become a Healing Touch practitioner, she learned how to trust her inner voice. She was now regularly working with invisible energy fields, so she got used to tuning in to what others could not see or hear. "It was my first time with an animal," she says. "And while people can tell me whether or not they are feeling better, dogs can't. So I knew I'd really have to listen to my heart and pay attention."

She worked on the dog for almost an hour, clearing, soothing, and harmonizing the energy vibrations she sensed around his paw. "His whole body was shaking, but he was licking my hand," JoAnn says. "I sensed he was saying, 'Oh, I'm so glad you're doing this; this feels so good.' I could feel his complete faith in what I was doing."

JoAnn knew when it was time to stop. "On a conscious level, I just knew that he would be fine," she says. "I just knew it." Then she went home.

The next morning, something truly wonderful happened. Her son called and said, "You have to come over right away." JoAnn raced over, and as soon as she walked in the house, the puppy jumped off a bench onto all four feet without any indication of pain or problems. "He's healed! He's healed!" her daughter-in-law cried, and they all hugged the little pup.

"Seeing was believing," JoAnn said later. "It was just incredible to see my efforts work."

☻ Love Light: The Touch of Love

Although you might not know anything about Healing Touch or have any desire to practice it, one thing is certain: A tender, loving touch can make wonderful things happen. The right kind of touch makes us feel safe and whole, free and at peace. When a parent puts an arm around a child's shoulder in praise or lovers knit their fingers together, a bond is created through which no harm can pass, if only temporarily.

Touch must be appropriate and welcome, but if you have some to give away, there is always someone waiting to receive it.

The difference your touch can make will warm your heart and those with whom you share it. And if you are in need of a soft and gentle touch, there are friends, family, support groups, and others who will gladly oblige with a hug or a hand to hold. Find your voice and ask for it. Or if you sense that someone else is in need of touch, offer some of your own gentleness, but only in ways that are acceptable to the other person.

Touch. Share the wonder of human warmth and kindness with others in your life.

Safe in Cyberspace

The wonder of sharing a lesson

*O*ur world is getting smaller. There are wonders in that, including the fact that we can share information in an instant that might have taken years to research before. But there are drawbacks, too. We now live in a global community, and not everyone is friendly or means to do well by us. Besides the conventional media like television, telephones, and ham radios, we are linked by the Internet. Although most people surf it without problems, some have experienced trouble they never wanted, either through viruses, spam, or, worst of all, harassment. In cyberspace, it is often difficult to identify an attacker, who can hide behind the anonymity of electronic transfer. But something wonderful happens when you decide to stand up and both be seen and heard.

"I WAS CYBER-SMART. I knew how to surf the Internet," seventeen-year-old Taryn says.

"My parents were protective of me. I didn't know the password to log onto the computer, so if I wanted to go on, I had to ask them. They also knew the passwords to all my e-mail accounts because I had nothing to hide. I just did some e-mail, looked up things for my school reports, and did some general surfing."

But one day, those safe activities turned dangerous. "I was checking my e-mail and got a message from a person called "I Hate Spicks," she said. "I was offended at this because I have Hispanic friends at school. So I opened up the e-mail, and inside was this hateful message calling me terrible names. It really, really hurt because I thought I didn't have enemies at my high school. So I called my mom to read it. She got on and told the person who wrote the e-mail to stop it or we would call the police. Then I logged off. We thought it would end there."

Unfortunately, it didn't. The next message to Taryn read: "I'm your worst nightmare. Your problems have just started." At that point, her parents called the sheriff's department, who later contacted the state attorney general for instructions on what to do. They preferred that Taryn stay on the Internet, as the only hope they had of catching the perpetrator was for him or her to make some kind of cyber mistake.

"I was just terrified," Taryn admits. "After the deputy sheriff left, we contacted our Internet provider and found out that it was someone local who was sending the message. That made school really hard for me, knowing it was someone from town."

Taryn, a straight-A student, was so distressed and distracted by her cyber stalker that her grades dropped. She hardly ate, slept, or talked, even though she is a very outgoing person. "My friends wanted to know what was going on," she says, "but the police asked me not to tell them. My home life was awful—I ran around locking doors and windows. I carried a cell phone and checked in with my parents every hour."

Then things went from bad to worse. "I started receiving pornography so vulgar that you wouldn't find it even in the worst magazine," she says. "But still, the police requested I stay online, hoping this person would make a mistake and they would get the break they needed."

Finally, they got one. "With the porn, there was a list of names, some of which we recognized. We gave this list to the police, and they brought the people in for questioning."

One boy confessed to the entire episode. Although that should have given Taryn some peace of mind, it didn't. "He was one of my best friends," she says sadly. "I trusted him and told him stuff I never told anyone else. It was a relief knowing who it was, but at the same time, it really hurt. He was given a restraining order for two years and a chance to apologize to me. He told me it was nothing against me, that his friends pressured him to do it. That really hurt, too, because it meant that other people thought it was funny."

Although the harassment was over, Taryn's problems were not. "Going to school was hard after that, because a few people gave me a difficult time for turning him in," she says. "I lost some friends, although most stood by me."

Then one day, something wonderful happened. "I felt sorry for myself for about a month and then decided I didn't want to wallow in self-pity," she explains. "I was working towards my Girl Scout Gold Award, which requires more than 100 hours of community service. I decided that creating a brochure would be the best way to educate people about Internet safety." Taryn turned to the Internet to do her research on how kids could protect themselves from cyber harassment, added wisdom gained from her own experience, and asked a graphic artist friend to help make sure the brochure was very businesslike.

When the brochure was completed, Taryn solicited funds from area businesses and clubs. She was hoping to print 1,000 brochures, but got enough money to print 10,000! They were quickly distributed to all the schools and law enforcement centers in Minnesota.

Then another wonderful thing happened. "My local paper featured me, and I received a call from a regional paper. I didn't want publicity because I was afraid I would get heckled by kids at school. But my mom talked to me, and we decided that by my getting interviewed, more people would learn how to be safe on the Internet." The piece turned out to be much larger than anyone expected and drew interest from a major Minneapolis newspaper.

"I was constantly reordering brochures because their article got picked up by the Associated Press, and newspapers from around the country featured my story. My mom was interviewed by a national magazine, too. Then CBS came to my school to interview me for *Investigative Reports*."

Within weeks, Taryn found herself on the speaking circuit, telling other students about Internet safety. Within two years, she had appeared at more than 150 schools in two states, and other schools in other states call regularly. To them, she sends a video of herself making her presentation.

Then another wonderful thing happened. Taryn received the Prudential Spirit of Community Award for Minnesota. She had to miss her junior prom to accept the award in Washington, D.C., but says the trip was worth it. "I met a hundred and three of the most incredible kids," she gushes. "There was one girl who tested wells in Florida for contamination and got legislation passed.

There was an eleven-year-old boy who had cancer five times, but managed to start a toy cart for other kids." (See "The Joy Cart.")

Taryn's project received a special Inspiration Award. When she received it, the presenter said, "Thank you for making something so terrible into something positive."

"I was trying hard not to cry, but I did break into tears," she says. "Then I asked all the other honorees who had not received awards to stand up, because their contributions made other people's lives better, too. And at that point, even the moms were crying. It was the most incredible moment of my life."

Taryn is now applying for scholarships so she can pay for her college education. "I want to go to American University in Washington, D.C.," she says confidently. "I want to be a public relations specialist, and I want to be where there are major news organizations."

By turning a terrible situation around, Taryn escaped from the shadows and now stands fully and bravely in the light. It's a wonderful place to be.

♥ *Love Light: Making Lemonade*

We all have heard the expression, "When life gives you lemons, make lemonade." Although Taryn admits that at first she felt sorry for herself, she says that when she changed her mind, everything changed for the better. She eventually found her true voice and made wonderful things happen.

What has made you feel small and afraid? If it's over and done with, what have you done with the experience you gained and the wisdom you now have? If you haven't already done so, share what you learned with a friend, a child, a support group, or other audience. There are many others who could benefit from what you know. Inspire others by showing them the wonderful way you've overcome adversity.

And if you'd like a copy of Taryn's Internet safety brochure, you can e-mail her at *Pream@wiktel.com* or call 218-681-5395.

The Joy Cart

The wonder of making a sick child smile

*I*t's tough for a child to be ill and just as tough on overwrought parents who often can do little more than stand by, feeling somewhat helpless as their child suffers. Although time and medicine can help, sometimes it takes a flash of surprise to bring a smile to a small ailing face.

That surprise can take many forms. As parents of hospitalized children can tell you, the hours drag on when a little one is confined to bed for days or even weeks on end. The arrival of an unexpected visitor or gift is usually welcomed with open arms. This change of focus offers a few moments of relief for both child and parent. In a dark and difficult time, that's wonderful.

JARRETT HAD CANCER FIVE TIMES before he was eleven years old, starting at age two and a half. While walking to the parking lot with his parents after a football game, he suddenly said his leg was tired and he wanted to be carried. Thirty-six hours later, he couldn't stand on it at all; and before the weekend was out, he was diagnosed with Ewing's sarcoma, a rare bone cancer.

He lost his lower right leg to the disease and underwent aggressive chemotherapy, but the cancer kept coming back. At age nine, he was diagnosed with myelodysplasia, a preleukemia condition likely caused by all the chemotherapy he'd had. Fortunately, Jarrett's younger sister Claire was a perfect bone-marrow match, and the transplant worked, at least for a while.

Shortly before his eleventh birthday, a biopsy revealed that the original Ewing's cancer had returned, and the treatment protocols began in earnest once more.

In spite of his disease, Jarrett never considered himself to be sick, and his parents decided early on to treat him as normally as possible. "From day one, we have treated Jarrett like he was going to live," his mother, Jennifer, says. "He is a functional part of this family. I schedule things for both kids to look forward to, like going to the bookstore or taking a short vacation when Jarrett feels well. We try to make the most of each day."

The night that Jarrett was first diagnosed, the retired priest from their parish came over to their house and said, "Jennifer, you've got to look for the good in this."

"I was furious," she remembers, "but I was raised to respect men of the cloth. But as the months and years go on, that has become our family motto. What we've done to keep the anger and frustration from eating us up is to look for the good in every day."

Jarrett, a bright and affable boy, started to counsel and mentor other cancer patients. "He's become a symbol of hope, even to adults," Jennifer says. "Seeing his determination really helps them to regroup." He is a real survivor. Within four days of one recurrence, he was back in school.

Then, during a thirty-eight-day stay in an isolated hospital room after the bone-marrow transplant, Jarrett made a decision. Three of the four walls of the nine-year-old's room were covered with cards from well-wishers. He had more toys than he would ever use. He looked at his mother and said, "Mom, I want to do something for the *other* kids in the hospital who don't have all the cards and toys I do. I want to start a toy cart."

"It wasn't the toy itself, it was the idea that someone you didn't know cared about you," Jarrett said later, recalling a previous hospital stay where a volunteer group known as the Pink Ladies delivered toys to the children each week. "It was something to look forward to. It would get your mind off your treatment. It always helped me get through my day. And I wanted to do it for all the kids at Children's Hospital."

Because of his vulnerability to infection after the transplant, Jarrett was not allowed to return to school immediately. His parents encouraged him to work out a business plan for his idea. So, rather than waste away the hours at home, he sat down, wrote out his goals, and created a list of action steps that would help him achieve them. He created a persuasive introduction letter and collected reference letters from people in the community who could vouch for him. He also got a letter from the board of directors of the hospital, endorsing the idea of the cart. Then he went around to friends, family, and area businesses to collect both toys and money.

Seven months after his long hospital stay, Jarrett and his Joy Cart were ready. The hospital invited the press to attend as he and his parents made the first deliveries to the children in the pediatrics area. Because Jarrett was vulnerable to disease, he could not enter the rooms of children with contagious conditions.

Mostly, he enjoyed the pleasure of seeing the children and their parents smile when they were offered a choice of any one item from the Joy Cart.

That experience alone was wonderful. But at the same time, something just as wonderful was happening. The hospital's public relations department had invited the media to cover the story, and an astounding number of reporters appeared. "We didn't expect anyone to show up since it was basketball time around here," Jennifer laughs, "but the room was full of reporters! By that night, the story had hit the Associated Press wire all over Kentucky."

Jennifer says that in spite of the initial burst of publicity, donations for the Joy Cart were a little slow at first. "But as word spread, churches, women's clubs, and Girl Scout troops wanted to get in on it," she noted. Then one day, Rosie O'Donnell called. Jarrett has been on her show twice. "She helped arrange for us to get a five-hundred-dollar monthly shopping spree at Toys 'Я' Us," Jarrett says of his famous friend. More recently, Jarrett appeared on *Oprah*, which sparked the creation of Joy Carts in hospitals across America by viewers inspired by his story.

In just fifteen months, Jarrett and his mother have delivered almost 2,000 toys to the pediatric patients in their local hospital. All of the children brighten up when they see Jarrett's toy cart coming. "One girl hadn't gotten off the couch all day," Jarrett says. "She had basically given up. But when she saw the cart, she jumped up and ran right over. It makes me feel really, really great to help kids like that."

Although he's not looking for praise, Jarrett has been made an honorary Rotarian and, like Taryn (see "Safe in Cyberspace"), has received the Prudential Spirit of Community Award. Every Tuesday, he leaves his friends at 4:30 P.M. to travel to the hospital with his mother for his Joy Cart rounds. Jarrett helps deliver the toys unless the recipient is contagious, in which case he waits in the hall while his mother does the work.

He intends to continue his life-improving work. "Our basement is full of toys, and so is a warehouse not far from here," he says. "We'd love to see other area hospitals served, so we're hoping more people volunteer." He's also working to inspire the creation of Joy Carts in other regions and countries.

Jarrett passed away in early October of 2002. Before he died, he had the pleasure of knowing that his desire to help other children was being fulfilled by Joy Carts that were launched in hospitals all over America.

☺ *Love Light: Spreading Joy*

When I got sick as a little girl, my mother would tuck me into bed, wheel in the television set from her bedroom, and then head downtown to buy me a toy. Although my sniffles and sore throats didn't instantly disappear when she walked in the door with a package gaily wrapped in polka-dotted paper, it always made me feel a lot better. Not only did I love the treat of getting a toy I didn't expect, I loved the fact that my mother cared enough about me to make the effort. In addition, while I was playing, I often forgot about my aches, pains, and sniffles.

Do you know a child who is sick? Surprise him or her with a quick visit and a little treasure, and watch something wonderful happen. Or if Jarrett's story has inspired you to want to start your own Joy Cart, make your list of contacts and get moving. For more information about Joy Carts, see *www.thejoycart.com*.

Without a Doubt

The wonder of invisible connections

Author Deepak Chopra once explained a wonderful scientific fact. He said that if you weigh a dying person, you might find, say, that he or she weighs 150 pounds. Curiously, after the person dies, the corpse will still weigh exactly 150 pounds! What this suggests is that whatever makes us alive and gives us our individual character is not a "thing." It has no weight or mass. It cannot be found, examined, or operated on in a human body, and yet we all know it exists. Most of us call this our soul or spirit; and religions, sages, and philosophers throughout the ages have suggested it doesn't die when our bodies do. Where, exactly, is the "person" inside our bodies, and where does it go when we die?

I use the words above in quotations because the following story suggests that even though our souls may leave our human containers, we live on. We talk about how the spirit goes to heaven, but we already know that heaven is neither over the rainbow nor in outer space. Which begs the question: What if heaven was right here among us? Perhaps it is a dimension of love and kindness that our dense forms and negative thinking prevent us from accessing.

That is, until love leads the way. For where there is love, wonderful things happen.

BROCK WAS AN OUTSTANDING ATHLETE. At sixteen, he stood 6'3" and had a "wingspan" of almost seven feet. Although he was only a sophomore, he played varsity basketball and was a champion rebounder. He had no trouble holding his own on the tennis court or football field, either. And there was more to Brock than sports. He was a straight-A student, taught religious school to third graders, and had a gorgeous singing voice. Plus, he was kind and thoughtful, and everyone who knew him loved him. "He was one of those one-in-a-million kids," his father says.

One day, Marshall, Brock's father, expressed annoyance at the messiness of his son's bedroom. Brock's reply was somewhat unusual. "Dad, I have a lot on my mind. I've had a vision from God that I'm not going to be here on earth for my eighteenth birthday. I don't know what's going to happen, but I have so much to do while I'm here that I can't be thinking about cleaning up my room."

Although Marshall tried to be reassuring, ten days later, Brock was killed in a freak automobile accident.

His family and community were overwhelmed with grief. More than 2,200 people attended Brock's funeral, which had to be held at the gymnasium at the high school. The day was dark and dreary, but at the end of the service, the first of many wonders appeared. "The sun came out and the whole place just lit up," Marshall said.

Without a Doubt

Although Brock left this earth in 1997, he has found ways to make his presence felt ever since. His family started experiencing too many "coincidences" to believe that they were anything but answers to their wish to remain close to their loved one in spirit.

The first was a picture the family found not long after Brock's death. In addition to his other skills, Brock was a talented artist and had drawn a picture of an angel that looked exactly like him. "It was as if he knew," his father said.

Brock's mother, Vicki, says Brock often comes to her in dreams. "The first dream was right after he died. Because of the accident, we didn't view the body, and I wish I had held his hand one last time. Brock had huge hands, and unlike most boys his age, he would still hold mine if we were sitting on the couch together." The night she made that wish, something wonderful happened. "I dreamt I was in the car, going to a football game. I looked in the backseat, and Brock was there. He reached over the seat and gave me his hand to hold."

A few months later, Brock's grandfather was out on the lake fishing. He was relaxed but thinking about Brock when suddenly his grandson appeared nearby, smiling at him. "There was no doubt it was Brock," he later told Vicki and Marshall.

Time did not diminish the evidence of Brock's presence. One year after Brock was killed, Marshall went down to his son's bedroom looking for some memento he could carry. "I wanted a piece of him with me," he says. Brock had a coin collection, so his father took a $2 bill and tucked it into his billfold. Later that day, Marshall went out to buy a half gallon of milk. The total came to $2.14. All he had in his wallet was Brock's $2 bill and a single. Reluctantly, he used the $2 bill to pay for the milk. But a few days later, he bought a round of drinks for friends. The total came to $17.80, and Marshall gave the waitress a twenty. He gasped with surprise when the waitress gave him two dimes and a $2 bill in change. "No one gives two-dollar bills as change," he says. "I knew Brock had a hand in it."

The next year, Brock's father was hospitalized with blood clots. A nursing student came into the room, and they began chatting. As they talked about their families, both of them started to cry when it came to the subject of Brock. Brock's father was awed once again when the student said she'd grown up on a farm located on the exact highway mile marker where Brock was killed.

Vicki not only continued to see Brock in her dreams, she found she could speak to him. "I had a dream I was sitting at a kitchen table with him," she explains. "He reached over and held my hand. So I asked him: 'How long do I have until I come to you?' And he answered, 'You can't come until your heart heals.' " Vicki knew he was referring to the mother of Brock's best friend, an old friend of Vicki's whom she had avoided since the funeral because the pain was too great. "I immediately called my girlfriend and apologized," Vicki says. "She was very welcoming and told me she had been reluctant to share the news that her dad was dying because of all we'd been through with Brock. But what she didn't know was that Marshall and I had wanted to find someone who was dying to give Brock a message for us. So we asked her father to tell Brock that we really miss him but we're trying really hard to make it here. Her dad was thrilled to get the message to deliver and died peacefully a week later. We went to the funeral, and my friendship with my girlfriend has never been better."

Vicki's dreams and conversations with Brock continued. Right before Christmas one year, Vicki asked Brock, "How long can you stay? It would really be nice if you could stay for Christmas." Brock answered, "Don't worry about Christmas. Christmas will be fine." "The next day, my mother called and said that my brother was coming home for the first time in eighteen years. We had a wonderful Christmas," Vicki says.

One time, Brock showed her a restaurant she'd never been to, filled with strangers and chafing dishes. On Mother's Day, she found herself walking into the exact place she'd seen in her dream. "If Brock hadn't died, I would have gone through life as a 'book Christian,'" she says, "someone who went to church and taught Sunday school but never lived the faith. I used to be very conservative and hang back. Through this, I'm a lot more daring about coming up to someone who's lost a loved one. I'm not afraid."

Both Marshall and Vicki know their son is near. On a trip to the state of Washington, they were admiring the scenery. "I was saying, 'Brock loved beautiful scenery so much. I wish we could have brought him here,'" Vicki says. Then Marshall went out on the deck of the ferry and took a picture. The couple had the picture developed that same day. Then another wonderful thing happened. "In the corner of the photo there is a gorgeous cross of light," Vicki says. "We were especially touched because it was Marshall's birthday."

There is little question in Marshall's mind that his son is an angel. The people of the town seem to think so, too. In Brock's memory, a high school service club decided to make angels and pass them out at the funeral service. "I only asked a handful of kids," the group adviser says, "and more than one hundred showed up to help!" The group made hundreds of angels from macaroni noodles and gave one to every family leaving the service. "I can take you to 200 homes in the area where people still have that angel hanging someplace," the adviser says. And today, the Lions Club sponsors a scholarship in Brock's memory for members of the service group. "He was tireless," she says. "He didn't know what the word 'no' was."

Brock's father has found the evidence of his son's presence comforting. "I've lost the fear of dying and the fear of disease," he says. "My son has given us the rare opportunity to know that we're here but for a split second. My values have changed since he died. Now I know that work is work, but family is everything. God is everything. Your priorities get straightened out fast when you lose a child."

"Brock wanted to save the world," he says. "What more can a young man do for people than show them he was close to God?"

☺ *Love Light: Listening to Heaven*

I am fortunate that my closest relatives are all alive and well here on earth. But I have lost beloved friends, and sometimes they will let me know they are nearby. One day I was driving down the highway, and my friend John's "theme" song came on the radio: "I Believe I Can Fly." I sat up and sang along, glad for a sweet reminder of him. As the song ended, a commercial began, so I randomly hit a button on the radio to change the station. The same song came on again, even though it is not in the Top 40 or on anyone's regular play list. That's when I knew that John was nearby, letting me know that all was well.

If you would like to connect with a loved one this way, try something very simple: Relax. Although sometimes angels come when you yearn for them, I have found that a more reliable way to get a sense of their presence is to relax or focus totally on something else. Then they can come to you in a way that you will understand and find comfortable.

Don't worry. You'll know when they are with you. And that's wonderful.

Lost and Found

The wonder of discovering a surprise helper

Too much of the time, we are afraid of life. We surround ourselves with stuff we believe makes us safe and comfortable, but it can disappear or be taken from us without notice. If and when it does, we feel vulnerable and frightened.

Ironically, these are the moments when something wonderful can enter. When danger makes the world seem fuzzy and intimidating, we have no choice but to let life help us in whatever way it can. When we do that, we can be surprised to find that assistance is everywhere, often in forms we never expected.

Rather than tell you a story from my own life, I will share this one, which I received via e-mail. Like many people, I receive a great many cyber messages. I have let my love for good stories be known, and as a result, many are forwarded to me. I do not know the original author of this story, but the person who sent it to me says it is true.

I like to believe that it is, because it reminds us that we are truly safe in this world. If we believe that, wonders happen.

"BRENDA WAS A YOUNG WOMAN who was invited to go rock climbing. Although she was scared to death, she went with her group to a tremendous granite cliff. In spite of her fear, she put on the gear and started up the face of the rock.

"She got to a ledge where she could take a breather. As she was hanging on, the safety rope snapped against Brenda's eye and knocked out her contact lens. There she was on a rock ledge, with hundreds of feet of rock cliff below her and hundreds more above her, and she couldn't see clearly. Frantically, she looked and looked and looked for her lost lens, hoping it had landed on the ledge. It wasn't there.

"Determined to reach the top, she mentally regrouped and finished the climb. Although she was uncomfortable without her one lens, she made it. When she reached the summit, she asked a friend to examine her eye and her clothing for her contact, hoping to be able to see clearly for her descent. Unfortunately, it wasn't there to be found. Brenda sat down, despondent, and waited with the others until the rest of the party made it up the face of the cliff.

"Her blurry sight made her more and more upset. Although her group would be descending the rock via a safe trail, she was far from home and had no way to replace her lost lens for the remainder of the trip. She dreaded the idea of not being able to see clearly for days. She began to feel desperate, which she knew was not a good state of mind for the rest of her planned adventure. So she prayed. She looked out across ranges of mountains, thinking about the Bible verse that says, 'The eyes of the Lord run to and fro throughout the whole earth.' She thought, 'Lord, You can see all these mountains. You know every stone and leaf, and You know exactly where my contact lens is. Please help me.'

"Brenda felt surprisingly calm during her descent. When she reached the bottom, something wonderful happened. A new party of climbers was just starting up the face of the cliff. One of them shouted out, 'Hey, you guys! Anybody lose a contact lens?'

"That would have been startling enough, but do you know why the climber saw it? An ant was moving slowly across the face of the rock, carrying it!

"Brenda says that her father is a cartoonist. When she told him the incredible story of the ant, the prayer, and the contact lens, he drew a picture of an ant lugging that contact lens with the words, 'Lord, I don't know why You want me to carry this thing. I can't eat it, and it's awfully heavy. But if this is what You want me to do, I'll carry it for You.' "

The e-mail ended this way: "I think it would probably do some of us good to occasionally say, 'God, I don't know why You want me to carry this load. I can see no good in it and it's awfully heavy. But if You want me to carry it, I will.'

"God doesn't call the qualified. He qualifies the called."

☺ *Love Light: Are You Qualified?*

Have you ever carried a load you felt was not your own, only to discover that in a way you could not understand, it served someone else perfectly?

This story has two wonders. The first is illustrated when Brenda trades her rapidly growing frustration for personal peace. Prayer is one wonderful way to do this, as we are actually releasing sound vibrations "right out of the horse's mouth" that prove we believe in a higher and greater power to help us. The instant we do this, we are connected to an invisible and loving stream of energy that is far more responsive than we can imagine. Tens of thousands of people around the world can tell their own stories of wonders that happen when we invite our Creator's generous flow into our lives. When we remember that we cannot always solve problems with our human faculties and give up the fight, wonder can enter.

The second wonder is illustrated by the father's cartoon of the ant. How many times have you felt that you carried a burden that was not your own, never knowing why you were the "chosen" one? Although it is gratifying to learn how and why our sufferings benefit others, that is not always possible. But if we believe that every piece of life experience fits some part of a much larger puzzle, wonders can happen.

Make Your Bed and Lie in It

The wonder of doing what you love

We've all heard the expression, "Do what you love, and the money will follow." The flipside of this is, "If you can't do what you love, love what you do." Either way, it's true that when work and love are synonymous, wonderful things can happen.

Further, work is often done with plans and projections. There are goals to meet, pathways to follow. While these are useful much of the time, they can limit wonder. When we think we know everything that is supposed to happen, it's difficult to allow something wonderful to surprise us. Some of the greatest wonders occur when we are willing to go the distance but don't have a predrawn map to get us there. The words "Can you help me?" open us to new ideas and directions that may be far better than any we could conceive ourselves.

LINDA WAS WORKING ON A NEWSPAPER, supervising telephone sales and doing research. She found herself eager for an exciting new direction and heard about a group in her rural town who were trying to create employment opportunities for women. Acting on faith and a sense of adventure, she quit her job and joined the board.

The group soon received a financial grant from the state to start a quilting company. Before long, they had employed a number of people to sew at home, and they were on their way. Linda was their marketing director, although she had more enthusiasm than experience. "We were so naïve," she says. "We thought we'd get the money, start the business, get our line into a catalog, and start counting orders."

When that didn't happen, Linda started knocking on doors. "People love to be asked to help," she says. "So I'd go in to see a buyer at a big-name department store and say, 'We need some help. Would you look at our products and tell us what you think?' Once they saw the quality of the work, they realized we weren't hicks producing some kind of church-bazaar-type products. The stores had buyers with a higher level of sophistication, and we had quilts for them."

Linda kept going out farther and farther geographically, which led her to the offices of a prosperous bedding store chain in Chicago. "Eventually, I ended up in the president's office. He invited me to their annual meeting in Hawaii. Soon after, we became a vendor that was included in all their regular meetings."

Business improved after that, but the small company was organized as a nonprofit entity, which was hard to sustain without new sources of funds. The company dissolved after five years, but Linda had found work she loved and was determined to stay in the fine-bedding business. "I was the only one from the company who had actually been out in the market," she says. "I knew I wanted to keep on, and I saw an opportunity to get into the custom-sewing business. The board gave their approval. When the quilt business ended, I decided I would start my own business."

Linda started her own enterprise with confidence that it would be profitable, since she had the basics in place. "My learning, my customers, and some of my sewers came from the previous business," she explains. For start-up cash, she used $2,000 that she had saved for a trip to Alaska, composed of $1,000 she had received from her grandmother and $1,000 that she had squirreled away over many years. "It was my own little stash," she says with a grin. When she invested it in her vision, something wonderful happened.

Soon after starting her new company, the president of the Chicago bedding stores told Linda about a hotel that wanted one thousand custom duvet covers. Linda's small business could never handle an order of that size, since buying the necessary fabric would be far too expensive. But then something wonderful happened: The president told Linda that the hotel was willing to supply the fabric. All she had to do was have it professionally sewn and deliver the finished products.

Linda jumped at the chance. "Things worked out perfectly. We had sewers from all over our area putting them together. To collect the finished duvet covers, my husband and I drove his old pickup truck on the dusty gravel roads to their farms. We'd bring the covers back into town and ship them from our garage."

That one order improved the cash flow of Linda's business dramatically, which gave her the ability to start introducing her own fabrics at the bedding store's meetings. Her desire to grow and learn remained high.

Then one day on an airplane, another wonderful thing

happened. Linda found herself sitting next to a woman whose husband was the marketing director for a well-known custom bedding line. "You know how you meet people on airplanes and they say, 'Come stay at my house?' " Linda asks. "Well, she did, and I went!" It was a great opportunity for her to share the wisdom of an experienced professional. "I learned all kinds of things about marketing high-end linens."

That led Linda to the furniture markets in High Point, North Carolina, where she says, "I felt like I belonged, right from the start." Linda quickly made friends with many of the designers. "I always felt happy in High Point," she says. "Some of the designers were attracted to that happiness, I think. I know that I smile a lot when I'm there."

Wonderful coincidences continued. In a High Point restaurant, Linda met designer Raymond Waites, who was doing a shoot for *Victoria* magazine. He needed some little pillows right away, and Linda was more than happy to oblige. She soon found herself creating an ever-expanding line of specialty pillows for him.

But all was not roses in Linda's cozy world. Shortly after she met Waites, she received a disturbing phone call that the Chicago bedding company she loved, trusted, and had served for years was filing for bankruptcy. "They owed us $13,000," she says sadly. "It was a major setback." Although Linda was upset, something wonderful happened when she called to share the bad news with her husband. "Scott's response was, 'Well, that's an awful setback, but you'll just have to work harder now,' " Linda recalls. "He didn't say, 'Well, that's too bad. You'll just have to pack it in.' I needed to have the support of my husband, and that proved to me that I had it." She heard exactly the words she needed when she needed them the most.

Linda kept going and growing. A decade or so later, her

company, Thief River Linens, now stocks 500 to 700 fabrics and has customers all over the United States and around the world. She is still a major home employer in her rural town. Her staff includes some thirty women who work out of their houses, in addition to another fifteen who work at the company's headquarters. Her company works with major national designers, creating luxury bed linens and pillows for furniture stores and designers. Linda travels around the world to find distinctive fabrics and enjoys wonderful relationships with mills in the United States.

"I've learned how lucky I am," she says cheerfully. "I have both a family and work I love."

Love Light: What's Love Got to Do with It?

When Linda quit her newspaper job, she wasn't thinking that she wanted to go into the high-end linen business. But she did love the idea of personal growth and a chance to work with a dynamic group of people, and she found both. That love fueled her through good times and bad, including when the nonprofit corporation folded and her biggest customer declared bankruptcy. Because of her love, not only of her business but of life itself, her company is sure to prosper in the years ahead.

So the question becomes: Do you love who you are as you're doing your current job? If not, how do you want to feel as you work? What kind of people do you want to surround you? What would make your life more dynamic and fun?

Close your eyes. That person is alive in you now. Make the decision to embrace him or her, and allow life to deliver a circumstance in which you can live that role.

Once you have the work that harmonizes with the person you want to be, leave the door open for wonder. Some of the most exciting and growth-producing moments in Linda's career happened not because she pursued them, but because she *allowed* them. She didn't go after that first huge order for duvets—it found her. Life will often do that when you are ready. Once the order came, she didn't brush it away by saying, "It's too big for me." Instead, she likely asked herself the wonder-producing question, "How can I make this work?" Once she fulfilled the order, she kept the wonders going by using her newly earned cash in ways that excited and fulfilled her.

Finally, a key in wonder-making is how we perceive setbacks. Although Linda was understandably upset when a major client went out of business, she embraced Scott's expression of faith and confidence. She didn't answer him sarcastically or brush him off. She knew she had been given what she needed to carry on. The next time life hands you a situation that wasn't what you thought you wanted or expected, ask yourself: "What part of me does this test? How committed am I to success? Am I ready to grow?"

Like Linda, you, too, can affirm that the path you are on is the right one for you. When you do, there is no limit to the wonders you can experience.

Strong Stuff

The wonder of achieving personal balance

Not all of us have the courage to quit our jobs and start over from scratch, as Linda did. She never had to battle child-care issues, an indifferent or difficult spouse, or concern about her basic survival needs. For many people, a reliable job with a steady income is critical for creating the peace of mind necessary to do anything else. That job doesn't have to be their life's passion; it just has to be something they can do well, with a good attitude, true ability, and knowledge. With that in place, they go out exploring paths that create a balance between passion and practicality, which leads them to wonder.

CAROL WAS A FIRST-RATE OPTOMETRIST. Her services were in great demand, and she was happy to work in an office several days a week. But no matter how many patients she saw or how many problems she fixed, she never felt totally fulfilled. Her husband was growing in his career, and her children were getting older and more independent. She felt she needed more for herself.

So whenever Carol wasn't in the office, she was enjoying the outdoors. She took long walks and even longer bike rides. She hiked and dug into her garden. Still, wonder was missing.

"I was searching for a physical niche, but I could not find it," she says. "One day, I picked up a copy of *Yoga Journal*, even though I wasn't practicing yoga at the time. I had taken a couple of beginners' classes, but I wasn't thinking it was for me. An article in the magazine talked about this book, *Power Yoga*, so I bought it." Eventually, Carol put the book on the reading stand attached to her NordicTrack and started reading. That's when wonderful things started happening.

"As I was reading this book, I got tears in my eyes," she says. "And I thought 'This is it!'" What she did next surprised even her. Carol, fairly shy by nature, picked up the phone and called the author. "I said to her, 'What is *ujjayi pranayama*?'" She laughs. "Over the phone, she's trying to teach me to breathe like Darth Vader." The conversation became electric. "I'm thinking, 'This lady is incredible,'" Carol says, "and I'm all fired up. I called her back a few weeks later and started asking her more questions." As Carol pursued her new passion, wonder entered. "She invited me to fly out, stay with her, and study yoga!" Carol gushes.

As a fortieth birthday treat to herself, Carol flew out and stayed at the author's home for five days, studying yoga. "The cost was absolutely minimal," Carol says. "She could have gotten an exorbitant amount but didn't ask me for anything."

Carol came home eager and ready to practice. As she pursued a daily routine, a sense of peace came over her. "I just felt like

'This is where I really need to be,' " she says. "This was what I was looking for my whole life."

Carol continued to practice optometry during the day and yoga at night and on her days off. She dedicated herself to mastering the physical discipline and, as she did, more wonderful things began to happen. "My body physically changed, and my mind started changing," she says. "I started reading more about meditation and focusing on the inner me." Carol's confidence increased, and she found it easier to make challenging life decisions relating to her job, her marriage, and her home. She amicably separated from her husband and started living independently with her children.

The more Carol practiced her yoga, the more her confidence grew. "I wanted to go to a different level," she explains. "Rather than having my practice just be me, I wanted to share it with other people. But I needed to learn the basics better so I could teach it."

A few months later, wonder struck again when the author called. "It would be good for you to be with other people and to learn from their experiences," she said. Carol was floored by what she then heard—her tuition would be free if she wanted to learn to be a teacher. "I had never specifically told her that I wanted to be a teacher," Carol says. "It was like she had read my mind and sensed this part of me that I wanted to share."

When Carol returned from her training, she started teaching yoga classes out of her home. That eventually evolved to Power Yoga classes in a local dance studio. "Now I have something I can actually focus on," she says proudly. "I know I always have my yoga to turn to when things aren't going as they should be. After I finish the practice, I always feel better and find that I gain better insights about what is going on in the rest of my life." Carol still practices optometry. She also practices and teaches Power Yoga.

She and her ex-husband remain friends, and her children are doing well in and out of school. She says that her yoga practice mirrors the rest of her life. "It's a lifelong challenge, because yoga isn't something where you perfect a pose. You can always keep moving forward with it." She has found her balance. "I challenge myself every day," she says. "And yet, I'm not in competition with myself. Yoga is about growth. And I'm growing all the time."

⑨ *Love Light: Get Physical!*

Carol's experience is a good example of the wonders that can occur when mind and movement find a livable balance. If you work in an office, factory, or other closed space all day, you can become overly focused on one aspect of who you are or what you are capable of doing. If you want something wonderful to happen, try balancing the intense mental work you do with something totally physical.

Professional athletes talk about being "in the zone," which is nothing more than complete absorption and surrender to what they are doing. Regardless of how much they might be sweating or grunting, they feel no pain and suffer no adverse aftereffects because energy is flowing to them and through them without resistance.

If you have never experienced such bliss, experiment. The simple fact is that our souls are walking around in physical containers that are designed to be used and enjoyed. If you need an intense stress-buster, try sports like running, rock climbing, or long-distance swimming. If you're the competitive type, choose a game—golf, tennis, soccer, basketball, bowling, hockey, or baseball. If smooth sailing is more your style, try dancing, rollerskating, or gliding on a manually powered scooter. If you like to keep things light, go to the playground and play hopscotch, climb the monkey bars, or swing on the adult-sized swings.

Carol must be extremely careful and delicate in all her movements when she is in the office, which is likely one of the reasons why Power Yoga works for her — it's in complete physical contrast with the rest of her day. Find what's fun for you and you'll find your perfect balance. When you do, you will likely find answers to some of the hardest questions in your life as well. And that's wonderful.

Getting Some Satisfaction

The wonder of finding personal peace

We live in a world in which nothing is ever good enough and we are never satisfied. Even when we have everything we think we should ever want, we are stirred by desire. Are we surprised, then, that so many people are restless and searching for something to quiet the untamed beast within? All too often, we think that the next partner or purchase will quiet the longings of our hearts and souls, but that is rarely the case. If anything, the call to wonder just increases when we discover that nothing external to ourselves ever penetrates much more than skin deep.

If we truly want to experience the life-sustaining peace of wholeness, we must come home to ourselves. We have to stop defining what we can do and be by what other people say is possible and make our own decisions. We must stop denying what is important and act on what recreates us in new and better ways. It is not always easy, but when we do, we are not the only ones who experience the wonders that result.

AT THIRTY-THREE, Alayne had accumulated many blessings: a great husband, beautiful son, loving family and friends, and the respect of her professional peers. But something was missing. Her parents had divorced when she was a teenager and barely spoke to one another. Her younger brother had died a few years before. When the company she had worked for was bought out, she was downsized out of a job. "I wanted peace, a sense of wholeness," she says.

Knowing she would not find it outside of herself until she found it inside, she made a choice. "After the birth of my son, who is named for my deceased brother, I wanted to be able to read from the Torah. So I decided to become a Bat Mitzvah."

Traditionally, simply passing the age of twelve for girls and thirteen for boys makes you a Bat (or Bar) Mitzvah in the eyes of the Jewish community. (Loosely translated, the term means "Daughter (or son) of the Covenant.") But most Jewish children spend years preparing for a special ceremony to mark the occasion, which includes reading from the Torah and leading the congregation in the major prayers. It is not easy to do this well, since the Torah, the sacred scroll that contains the five books of Moses in their original Hebrew, is written without vowels. In addition, the Torah reading is always followed by a Haftorah reading, which is chanted. Again, learning the "trope" or melody of the characters is no easy feat.

Alayne had little religious training as she was growing up. "When I was twelve, my parents gave me the option of going to Israel for a month or having a formal Bat Mitzvah," Alayne says.

"I chose Israel because I didn't want to sing Hebrew in front of a huge group of people." She laughs. "And I wanted to take a month off from school and get a tan!" Alayne traveled with her grandparents, who refused to let her sit by the pool and, instead, took her to all of Israel's major religious sites and cities. "Every year I realize more how valuable that trip was to me," Alayne says. "I refer back to it so often, it feels like it was yesterday."

Determined to answer the call of her soul, Alayne made the commitment to attend a Bat Mitzvah class for eighteen months. With freelance work and a toddler, finding the time wasn't easy. Nor was convincing her family of her desire. "My whole family didn't take it seriously," she says, "but I did. I went every Wednesday night for one and a half years. My husband isn't Jewish and didn't really understand what a Bat Mitzvah was."

Alayne's Torah portion was no picnic, either. Her responsibility was to read the Hebrew flawlessly, find personal meaning in it, and relay her observations to others. But there was a problem. "It was boring," she says, "from the book of Numbers. It was all about Moses taking the census. Needless to say, when I first read it, the spiritual lightning bolt did not come from the sky to enlighten me. Frankly, I could barely read the English translation without a big yawn."

Alayne tried to look at it from Moses' point of view. "Imagine trying to count six hundred thousand hot, tired, cranky people," she says. Even with a more lighthearted approach, she wasn't satisfied. Finally, she asked an acquaintance to help her interpret it. That's when something wonderful happened. He saw the portion from an entirely different point of view, which changed Alayne's perspective. "He said it's not about counting; it's about an entire people committing to God for the first time and the holiness that was added to their lives because of that," she noted. "*Ahhhh!* That was the lightning bolt I had been waiting for. I had already made my own commitment. Now I just needed to find the holiness."

Alayne's confidence grew as she continued her studies. Her commitment paid off: "Instead of being scared to sing the words of Torah, I thought, 'I have a voice!'" she says. "Here I was, singing the Torah in Hebrew in front of people I didn't even know." She, her family, and her friends were all delighted by her spiritual leadership.

But it was later, at the meal she had lovingly prepared for her guests, that happiness turned to wonder. "My whole family was there. Although we had been together physically many times, it was the first time it felt like we were together both physically and emotionally, with love present. I thought that might have happened at my wedding, when my brother died, or when my baby was born, but it didn't. Instead, it happened at my Bat Mitzvah.

"My parents spoke to one another, and some peace came out of it. And I was surrounded by my in-laws, my grandparents, and friends I truly cherish," she says.

As Alayne looked at all of them, another wonderful thing happened. "I realized I have all these people around me and I am so blessed," she says. "I also thought of all the people who weren't there, including my brother and others who had died but lived on in our hearts and through our actions. I started getting mushy about all of them, but then I reminded everyone that all too often, we go through life feeling certain things about people we love and telling everyone else *but* them." She paused. "Holiness to me is drawing people close and telling them we love them."

The wonderful thing that happened that day was that Alayne ended one chapter of her life and began another. "It was like a period at the end of a sentence," she says. "I feel totally new and peaceful. It's like the first thirty-five years prepared me for what I feel now, which is joyous. I have not slept through the night since the Bat Mitzvah; I have this feeling that there's so much urgency to live fully in every moment." And that's wonderful.

❀ *Love Light: Deciding for Yourself*

When we are children, we live by others' decisions—our parents, our teachers, and other authority figures. Although we can get drafted and vote at eighteen and drink when we're twenty-one, there's really no date or time when we know for certain that our decisions are our own.

If you make the same decisions over and over, they become beliefs. Some people spend their entire lives living by other peoples' decisions. But it doesn't have to be. We always have choices about what we do and how we see things. When Alayne acted on her convictions and opened her perspective to new ideas and ways of seeing things, she found the wholeness she had been seeking. The wonder of personal peace occurred when she decided for herself what was valuable and true.

You don't need a religious ceremony or a rite of passage to do this. Just choose any area of your life that is important to you and ask yourself, "What decisions have I made about this? And are they truly my decisions or someone else's?"

Then, act on what you know. Do or say something that confirms what you believe. Don't worry if you will have the time, the stamina, or the money to do this. When personal truth leads the way, wonders happen.

Wake-Up Call

The wonder of escaping a long, bad dream

When I was a child, my grandfather had a stroke. He regained his ability to move and eat but talked so slowly that it could take him five minutes or more to get out a full sentence. It was as if he existed in a semi–dream state and would come out of it only briefly to communicate with us. We always wondered how much of our rapid-fire conversation he understood or cared to understand.

It is difficult to live between two worlds, a problem faced by every person who has ever had a complicated or debilitating illness. Sometimes the mind works perfectly, but the body will not cooperate. Other times the body functions normally, but the mind is lost. We want to participate in life, but we do not fit, and others do not always know what to do with us or how to respond. If our brains and/or bodies could speak when we cannot, physical wonders might happen. In the meantime, sometimes a change of environment can produce a change in perspective that can set something wonderful free.

TWENTY-THREE-YEAR-OLD CANDY had the worst headache of her life. She lay down on the living-room couch while her sister went to fetch some meat for dinner but soon felt as if she was going to vomit. She headed for the bathroom but was so dizzy that she lost her balance and fell. She managed to crawl into the kitchen and tried to yell for help, but only moans came out of her mouth.

When her sister returned, she started asking Candy hysterically what had happened and what was wrong. "My eyes were huge," Candy remembers, "and all I could do was mumble. The whole right side of my body was paralyzed."

An ambulance was summoned, and Candy slipped into a coma. Almost ten months would pass before she remembered what happened that fateful Thursday afternoon.

Candy was hospitalized in a city that was more than an hour away from her rural town. The doctors diagnosed her condition as a ruptured arteriovenous malformation and said only time would tell whether Candy would live or die. They performed a tracheotomy to reduce the chance of a lung infection, and Candy's coma lifted slightly. She was able to respond to verbal commands; and before long, she opened her eyes, although she did not seem to see anything around her. A month passed, and Candy became more physically active, throwing off her covers and grabbing the bed rails, but she still couldn't talk.

Candy remembers how she felt while in the coma. "I knew I was in a dream, and I was starting to realize I was having a hard time waking up. Everything was so make-believe. The place I was in felt like a mixture of Heaven and Oz. People I did know looked different to me, and there were so many people I didn't know. I thought God was having me dream this and that everyone had this type of dream, but then you woke up and would not remember any of it."

Eventually, frustrated with this surreal dream world, Candy tried to ask, "When will I wake up?" All that came out of her mouth was the word, "Winter." Since it was July at the time, her family laughed. "I was so upset by all this," she remembers. "All I could imagine was how fun this dream had started out and how now it was turning into a nightmare. I started wondering: Did I miss the cue to wake up?"

Candy began to ask God to please help her wake up. "I prayed and sang, but of course, no one could hear me," she says. She was half-aware of the outside world and realized that the nurses had to put bibs on her to feed her. She was mortified. "I just wanted to wake up," she says.

Friends, clergy members, and family visited often, bringing Candy's favorite albums and taking her down to the music room so they could play the piano for her. Nothing bridged the gap between Candy's awareness and her physical world. Days and weeks passed, and Candy became more and more aware of the limitations of her body and her surroundings. Out of frustration, she became less and less cooperative with her nurses, doctors, and therapists. They finally gave up, saying there was nothing more they could do for the young woman, and made arrangements to have her transferred to a smaller hospital in her hometown.

When they did, something wonderful happened. Candy's restlessness disappeared. "I realized I was back in my home town," she says. It was where she knew she belonged. With her environment changed, her perspective changed as well. "They brought me there on a Friday, and it still felt like it was a dream.

But I knew without any doubt that I would wake up on Monday."

Visitors came and went throughout the weekend, but Candy wouldn't speak to them. Just two short days later, in the wee hours of Monday morning, Candy experienced a physical shift. "Finally, I knew this was real life and that I was safe," Candy says, and her dream state disappeared. She started talking, and a nurse heard her speak. "She stayed with me for about an hour," Candy remembers. "I was scared. I didn't dare go back to sleep because I was afraid I'd go back into the coma."

The hospital summoned Candy's family, and quickly her mother, brother, and sister came over to be with her. "I couldn't tell them I was in a dream that whole time," Candy says. "All I could do that first day—even that first month—was cry. After you have a stroke, your emotions are completely turned around."

After that, time passed slowly for Candy. It took her more than two and a half years to relearn how to walk, talk, eat, and take care of herself again. After her therapy was complete, she became a volunteer for an occupational development center. The stroke left her legally blind, with double vision, short-term memory loss, and a weak right side. But it did not diminish her love for life. She eventually met and married a kind, considerate, loving man and had two children. Candy's husband took paternity leave from his job to help care for the children after delivery, and her mother and in-laws offered two months of their own time after that.

Today, almost twenty years later, Candy says, "I feel now that this is the way it was meant to be. Every so often I get upset, especially because I don't have a driver's license. And then I see people in wheelchairs and feel glad I can walk. I've learned to accept things." That's wonderful.

❀ *Love Light: Just What the Doctor Ordered*

When someone we love has a stroke, goes into a coma, or struggles with any other serious illness that impairs his/her ability to communicate, it's all too easy to assume that he or she is "out of it" and cannot see, hear, or understand what is happening. As Candy's experience clearly illustrates, this is not necessarily so. Her parents and friends knew that and did everything they could to speak to and interact with her in as normal a way as possible, even when she did not respond for months.

If you have someone in your life who is struggling in this way, try weaving together a comfortable security blanket of familiar pictures, items, and activities you know he or she likes.

Stay focused on the person's "normal" life, not the limitations brought on by disease. Always walk in with a smile and a calm and confident manner, and speak to your loved one as you normally would. You might be surprised to learn later that your words and actions were "just what the doctor ordered."

Or, as in Candy's case, you might try moving the patient to a more familiar environment. Candy said that when she got to her local rural hospital, she knew she was "home" and felt safe. From that perspective, she had the sense that it was all right to come out of her coma. If your loved one is not physically able to come home to his or her own house, you could consider refurbishing as much as possible of his/her hospital or nursing home room with personal effects.

Whatever happens, be patient. It is never easy to deal or live with someone who is living between two worlds. Nurture your own spirit so you have the strength, confidence, and support you need to keep open the possibility of wonder.

A Circle of Love

The wonder of community support

The phrase "It takes a village to raise a child" has become popular these days. This is never truer than when someone is sick. Not only is the patient stressed, but so are the full-time caregivers, who are often family members trying to juggle multiple responsibilities. If ever a wonder is needed, it's during a long, slow recovery or decline.

In "Wake-Up Call," we learned that Candy received plenty of love, support, and visits from family and friends. Their demonstration of affection went on patiently and continuously for months. This was in addition to the quality care and comfort she received in not one, but two hospitals. Her story does not reflect the devastation of being sick and alone, which may be why something wonderful happened. For when spirits join together, life changes for the better.

The plain and simple fact is that fear makes a hasty exit when love is around. A small circle of love can grow very, very large in a hurry. When that occurs, wishes come true and wonders happen.

CHAD STARTED HAVING TROUBLE walking when he was three. His doctors soon diagnosed his problem as an aggressive form of muscular dystrophy and warned Chad's parents that their middle child would likely die during his teen years.

In spite of that dire diagnosis, Chad and his family did everything they could to live normally. He joined the Cub Scouts. He took piano lessons and played the xylophone in the school band. In high school, he joined the choir and was made honorary football captain.

Chad treasured his independence and, as a young boy, rode his bike everywhere until his legs became too weak to pedal. Not long after he received a manual wheelchair, his older brother raced him down the halls at school until Marie, their mother, caught them. Before she could say a scolding word, however, Chad grinned and said, "So that's what it feels like to run!"

By the time he was eight years old, however, Chad's muscles had deteriorated to the point where he needed an electric wheelchair. Despite the fact that both of his parents were employed, the family's medical insurance covered little of the $7,000 cost. Fortunately, the local Muscular Dystrophy Association chapter was able to help, and Chad was soon on the go again.

"The first thing he wanted to do was take himself to the Dairy Queen," Marie remembers. "When I asked how he intended to get in the front door, he said, 'Don't worry, Mom. I'll go through the drive-up!' " With his mother following close behind him, Chad had a renewed sense of freedom and accomplishment . . . and a chocolate shake.

But the 350-pound wheelchair was too heavy to transport, especially since the family had neither a ramp to get it into their house nor one to load it into their vehicle. Charlie, Chad's father, and Marie found it difficult to pay for a lift on their salaries as teachers. So more often than not, Chad had to be carried in someone's arms or pushed along in his old wheelchair. The family never complained but held the wish for greater ease and freedom in their hearts. Heart-to-heart, their friends heard the unspoken song, and it wasn't long before something wonderful happened.

"The president of the Education Association called me," Marie explains. "She said, 'We'd like to have a fund-raiser for Chad.' We had never thought of that, even though we had participated in events like that for other people. We were grateful and very much in awe."

It didn't take long before "Give Chad a Lift!" became the loving battle cry of the entire town. The regional Aid Association for Lutherans agreed to match whatever money was raised during two area fund-raisers: a potluck hosted by the local United Lutheran Church and a pancake-and-sausage breakfast held at the town's high school by the Education Association. The entry to both events was a free-will offering, and many of the checks were for far more than the meal was worth—often $50 or $100. The Boy Scouts held a raffle for a special rag doll. Eight independent basketball teams from around the area created a tournament in the afternoon, with the proceeds going to Chad's fund. After the event, the players from the winning team all crowded around Chad to give him their trophies as souvenirs of the day.

The events raised $10,000; and before long, Chad was independently navigating the new ramp built on the front of his family's house as well as the lift the family was able to install in their van. The leftover funds went to pay more of Chad's medical expenses and to buy him a television so he never had to miss a Chicago Bulls game again. "Chad's father and I were shocked, pleased, and grateful," Marie remembers.

Chad's spirit and his determination never waned, in spite of the progression of his disease. Wonderful things continued to happen. In his sophomore year in high school, he was named "Cardinal of the Week" because of his high academic standing in biology, his great school spirit, and his good appearance. Not long after that, the Make-a-Wish Foundation sent him to meet Scottie Pippen, then of the Chicago Bulls, a lifelong dream.

After Chad's eighteenth birthday, however, the family knew it would be his last Christmas. He was hospitalized in January during a trip out of town to see his brother play college basketball. Once again, the United Lutheran Church had a free-will offering, matched by the Aid Association for Lutherans fund. A local newspaper wrote a story, and suddenly gifts started appearing from friends, family, and total strangers. "Chad received sixty balloons, more than three hundred fifty cards, three faxes, gifts, money, and hundreds of phone calls," Marie remembers. "And he enjoyed each and every one."

On March 8, 1999, Chad died. His funeral was held at the high school to accommodate the more than 800 people from the area who wanted to attend. The high school football team came in uniform, and the letter Chad received for his work with the football team was on display.

His three award books, a poem a friend had written for him, and his wheelchair were visible also. Chad was buried wearing his authentic Bulls warm-up jersey, and a five-year-old friend placed a Michael Jordan basketball card in his casket beside a three-leaf clover left by his uncle in recognition of a donation made to the Muscular Dystrophy Association.

Today, there are memorials to Chad all over his small town. "God gave us Chad as a gift," his mother says tearfully. "We gave to Chad, he gave to others, and others gave to others because of him." Monies the family received after the funeral have helped more than a half-dozen organizations.

"We miss Chad a great deal," she says. "It's hard. But living within the circle of love he left behind eases the pain tremendously." That's wonderful.

☻ *Love Light: Give It All You've Got*

It's funny, but people can be stingier with love than with money. The amazing thing about Chad's story is that everyone in it just let his or her love flow. No one stopped to measure how much he or she was giving or wondered whether what was done was the right thing. They just poured their hearts into every effort, and the results speak for themselves. They expected nothing but received every wonder imaginable. Goals were met, a family was liberated, and everyone enjoyed good times.

Right now, there is probably someone who could use your unconditional love. Express it however you feel most comfortable—with time, support, a card, a fax, a check, or applause. Never worry if it is the right thing or if it is enough. Just open your personal gates of resistance, and let the love flow. Invite others to join you. Have fun, and keep your mind on life, not disability or illness. Pay attention, because if you stop to notice, you'll see sickness and the limitation it brings disappear, if only for a little while. That's the most wonderful thing that can happen.

Family Surprise

The wonder of discovering loved
ones you never knew you had

I am fortunate to have two brothers, so I've never wondered what it would be like to grow up without siblings. Part of learning to define myself was in contrast to the things they said and did, and I can't imagine how different I might be if they were not in my life.

I know plenty of only children, however, and they tell me that while they never got in trouble for playing chicken with their younger siblings, they sometimes wished they had a family peer who could share the ups and downs of life with them. They wanted to see themselves and their lives through someone else's eyes. For an only child who is adopted, that yearning is even stronger.

Part of our perspective on who we are and what we can or cannot do comes from our family. If that family turns out to be far larger or different than what we originally thought, wonders can happen.

ARDELL WAS ADOPTED when he was three weeks old. His biological mother had spent each precious day they had together loving him, naming him, and having him baptized. She didn't want to give him up, but as a single, teenaged mother in the early 1920s, she had little choice. Fortunately, his adoptive parents cherished him, and he grew up happily as their only child.

After they died, Ardell felt a void that nagged at him constantly. "I wonder if I've got parents someplace," he said to his wife, Tess, one day. "Well," she said, "your mother's name is on your birth certificate. Why don't you try to find out?"

They traveled to the heritage center in the state capital and found Ardell's birth records. Everything matched what little they knew to be true, and there was more they did not know. "It was an overwhelming moment," Tess remembers. "We looked at each other and said, 'Could this really be happening?' "

Ardell discovered that his mother had died in 1969. His biological father had passed away decades earlier at a young age. From marriage records, they discovered that his mother had gotten married not long after giving Ardell up for adoption, not to his biological father, but to another young man from a nearby farm. With more research and contact work, they found out that the couple had moved to Iowa and raised ten children there. When Ardell and Tess left the state capital, he wondered if he would ever meet his siblings.

It didn't take long to find out. Ardell, a minister, called friends in the area of Iowa where his biological family supposedly resided. He told these contacts that he was in search of his family there. They immediately offered to help Ardell in his search. "They told us they had genealogists in their church and offered to contact us if they found out anything," Tess says. It wasn't long before something wonderful happened.

In just a few hours, the phone rang. It was one of the genealogy helpers. "I think your sister lives close to me," he said. He asked Ardell several questions and then proceeded to write a letter to each of the brothers and sisters telling them about their newfound brother.

Ardell did not know that the genealogist had sent letters to the siblings. All he knew was that he wanted to travel to Iowa to learn more. He and Tess left home shortly afterward, although not without some trepidation. "We were nervous," Tess admits. "If these were Ardell's siblings, it would have been very easy for them to reject us."

They soon discovered that their fears were unfounded. Seeking reassurance, Ardell contacted the friend who had gathered the genealogists. Happily, his friend told Ardell that his older sister was waiting for them. But when Tess and Ardell drove up, the reception was more precious than either of them could imagine. "She came out of the door with her arms open and said, 'Welcome, brother. We've been waiting for you,' " Tess says. "It was wonderful."

After that, the wonders kept coming. Within a few minutes of their arrival, several more siblings came. Ardell and Tess eventually met all ten siblings and their families. They stayed in the area three days to get better acquainted, and by the third day, one of his new family members had made a computer banner and hung it above a doorway in his sister's house that said, "Welcome to our family."

"They could have thought of him as an intruder, but they embraced him with open arms and we knew we were accepted," Tess says.

After that, the wonders never ceased for what remained of Ardell's life. He was an accomplished pianist and singer, skills that his family and countless friends admired. "I once said to him, 'Honey, there has to be someone in your background who passed this gift on to you,' " Tess says. As Ardell was playing his mother's piano at his sister's house, she leaned over and told him, 'You know, our mother played the piano every day and sounded just like that.' " In addition, Ardell's mother had five sons and made known her wish that one of them go into the ministry. Ardell, her first-born, was the only one who did, although she never lived to know that.

Visits between Ardell, Tess, and his newly enlarged family continued. The family enjoyed a big reunion in 1996 with more than 130 people attending. The group was so large that it was difficult to get everyone to church services by 8:30 A.M. "The minister there suggested to us, 'Ardell and both of his sons are ministers, and your family makes quite a congregation, so why don't you just hold your own service?' " Tess remembers with a laugh. "So that's what we did!

"Ardell used to say to me, 'Now I know my roots.' He was just so thrilled and happy about it," Tess says. When he died in 1999, several of his brothers and sisters traveled to the funeral. "I feel that he died a happy man," Tess says. "We have three children, nine grandchildren, and many great-grandchildren in addition to his brothers and sisters and their families. After we met the rest of his biological family, he would often sit in his easy chair in the family room and say, 'Oh, Tess, I have to be one of the happiest men in the world.' "

☯ *Love Light: Back in Touch*

Not everyone's adopted, nor does every biological family of an adoptee wish to be found. But almost all of us have friends who influenced who we were, what we did, or who we have now become. Is now a good time for you to see yourself through their broader perspective or for you to see them through new eyes?

If love, memories, or wistfulness begin to call you, go searching. Thanks to computer databases and the Internet, it is relatively easy to find people these days. You might try the database of your hometown high school directory or the alumni association of the college or university your friends attended. You can look for a name and address in one of the white pages directories online if you have an idea of what city and state your friends might live in. If those don't take you where you want to go, try looking for hints in any of the news databases online.

If the love between you was strong, they will likely be thrilled to hear your voice again. Ahhh . . . wonderful!

Goal for It!

The wonder of inspiring others

When children begin to speak, we encourage them. "Oh, how wonderful! Talk more, talk more!" When they do, we fan their abilities by saying, "Isn't he clever? Isn't she adorable?" But somewhere around their third or fourth birthdays, all that changes. What was once considered laudable gets severely limited: "Keep quiet! This isn't the time to talk!"

By the time we are adults, surveys show that most of us would rather die or have root canal surgery than speak in public. The fear of looking stupid, ill-prepared, or just plain nervous holds many people back from expressing some of the dynamic energy they have inside themselves. Our worries keep wonders away. We never know how we might inspire others unless and until we stand up and speak out.

"LEADERSHIP CAMP WAS A LITTLE overwhelming at first," Johnny remembers. "I wasn't feeling well, and I could be a little intro-verted—you know, sitting in the back row, that kind of thing." Fortunately, the seventeen-year-old had packed the confidence gleaned from his strong academic abilities, cross-country track successes, and practice with the extemporaneous speaking team. His teachers had recommended him for the one-week camp spon-sored by the Rotarians, where he was supposed to hone his lead-ership skills and develop a personal vision for his life.

Johnny came with an open mind. "I didn't have a whole lot of expectations," he admits. "I thought it would be casual, like summer camp." He was surprised by what he found. More than 100 eager, enthusiastic students from four states and several coun-tries had gathered for the experience. "It was a very active, engaged group," he says. "My immediate impression was that my co-campers were terrific. I had never been in a group of students that had been as active as I was before."

Two days into the camp, Johnny felt better physically and was better adjusted mentally. "I became more involved and out-spoken," he says. One of his assignments was to develop a personal mission statement. "It didn't have to be a hard and fast statement, but rather more of where I wanted my life to go," he says. The campers were told that their statements should answer four impor-tant questions: Is it the truth? Is it fair to all concerned? Does it build goodwill and better friendships? Is it beneficial to all?

"I was a bit undecided about tangible goals like an occupa-tion," Johnny says. "So instead I focused on how one seeks to achieve one's goals rather than on the goal itself." The camp was divided into groups, and the directors said that one person from each group would be able to present his/her vision at a gathering two days later. Johnny volunteered for his group. He worked on his speech day and night. When the other students were relaxing during recreation time, Johnny was busy working on his outline.

When the fateful night came and it was his turn to take the podium, Johnny felt butterflies in his stomach. "I had never given a speech to people I didn't know well," he says. "It was as big an audience as I'd ever spoken to." He relaxed the group by pointing out that the longest speech in American history was a twenty-four-hour–plus filibuster by Senator Strom Thurmond. "If you get anxious while I'm speaking, remember that my speech will be relatively short by comparison—a mere six or seven minutes." Everyone laughed.

As they did, Johnny relaxed, too. His outline lay on the podium before him, but he found he didn't need it. He spoke straight from the heart. "I talked about some of the things I thought we learned from camp, including being involved with new people," he says. For his vision, he quoted Archimedes: "Give me a lever and a place to stand, and I will move the world." "I told them that, figuratively, what we had learned was like the lever we could use," Johnny says.

His oral mission accomplished, Johnny was satisfied. That's when something wonderful happened.

The audience was on its feet, applauding. For all his public speaking practice, Johnny had never brought an audience to its feet before. He was surprised and delighted and came away from his camp experience with a heightened self-confidence and an eagerness to rouse such enthusiasm again. "That day, I crossed a threshold. It was extremely important prior to my senior year of high school," he says. "It was the first time in my life that an audience was applauding for me and my ideas rather than for the event itself. It caused a permanent change in me."

Johnny graduated as the valedictorian of his class. He was

chosen to speak during the graduation ceremony, this time to an audience of almost 1,500 people. Once again, he quoted Archimedes, and again he brought the audience to its feet.

Today, Johnny is considering a career in public speaking. "I want to be in a job that involves communications and exchanging ideas," he says. Then he laughs. "I'm a lot less introverted with groups than I used to be."

☺ *Love Light: Say It Again, Sam!*

Words are very powerful things. They can hurt or heal, depending on how we use them. Even if you are not a public speaker like Johnny, you do talk to others every day. We take most of these exchanges for granted, but we shouldn't. As author Stephen Covey points out, every encounter is like a bank transaction—we are either putting something in or taking something out. If we become aware of how our chosen words are making others feel, we can build up enormous reserves of goodwill. Plus, with kind, enthusiastic words, we affirm the value of those closest to us.

So start paying attention to what's coming out of your mouth. Most of what we say is based on the 80 percent of our thoughts that are negative. We are constantly criticizing, judging, and limiting what we are experiencing. Is that really the perspective from which you want to create your life?

Before you speak, do what good public speakers do. Decide what you want to say and what point you're making by saying it. Pay attention to your tone, your choice of words, your facial expressions and gestures, for they can contradict or enhance anything that comes out of your mouth. You don't need an outline for every conversation—just a willingness to uplift others and yourself. Focus your words on what is meaningful to the other person rather than just talking about yourself or reacting to what he/she is saying.

As you become more aware of your speech, you'll be amazed at what can happen. Words carry very powerful subatomic vibrations that are like little magnets, drawing to you whatever is most like them in character, tone, and intention. If you want wonders to happen, choose your words carefully.

A Precious Prophecy

The wonder of knowing what will come next

*M*illions of people read horoscopes every day, hoping to get a sense of what might happen to them. We want to be prepared in case life might throw trouble our way. We want to be in control. We want everything to work out perfectly.

Sometimes that happens, but it's usually not because we forced things to obey our stubborn, unyielding wills. Something wonderful happens when we know with certainty and confidence that we are connected to a loving, responsive universe, that ultimately there is nothing to fear, and that somehow things will turn out all right in the end.

A few lucky souls live from the heart, expecting the best and often getting it. When life keeps its promises without our even having to ask, that's wonderful.

DEXTER WAS TWENTY-FOUR YEARS OLD and ready for adventure. He had just been released from four years of service in the U.S. Navy and wanted to visit friends in Spokane, Washington. He lived in Los Angeles and had no suitable means of transportation. But he didn't let that stop him. In 1972, everyone seemed filled with leftover love and goodwill from the freewheeling 1960s. So Dexter decided to hitchhike.

A friend came to his house to say good-bye. "Where will you sleep tonight?" she asked, concerned for his well-being.

Dexter let his spirit answer the question. "A rich woman will give me a ride, and I'll stay with her."

"My response just popped out," he says. "At the time, I didn't feel any attachment to it. I just experienced it as a pleasant fantasy, a prediction that somehow I knew would come true."

So Dexter hit the road. The day he left was beautiful, warm, and sunny. He got one ride, then another and another, but none turned out to be the rich woman he had imagined in his prophecy. "I let some cars pass me by," he says casually. "I was just happy to be on the road, whether I got a ride or not. I just knew that all was well and that the cars that passed me by *should* pass me by. That was the only way I'd be there for the one who was supposed to give me the experience that had flashed into my mind."

Before long, something wonderful happened. A woman in a midnight-blue Buick Park Avenue pulled over, and Dexter hopped in. "There were two others in her car," Dexter says. "So I wasn't immediately thinking that this was the woman of my prophecy."

The foursome rode on for two or three hours, chatting casually. When everyone was feeling comfortable and relaxed, the woman turned to Dexter and asked if he wanted to stay at her vacation home on the coast before continuing his journey.

"That's when I realized that my prediction had come true!" Dexter says.

Dexter did, indeed, stay at the woman's beautiful coastal home that night. The three-bedroom house was set on the edge of a cliff with the ocean surf pounding below. She left the next day but asked him to stay for a few days and care for the place until she returned. She gave Dexter some cash for necessities and the use of her spare car.

"It seemed unreal and magically wonderful," he says. "I stayed for a few days and then moved on. I never heard from her again."

Dexter continued to hitchhike for the next year, but he never again made another prediction. He didn't have to. "I met many helpful, kind people during that year," he says. "And I always knew that what was happening should happen. I didn't care whether that meant being passed by for hours on end or being picked up. It was a magical time — I just enjoyed the ride life was giving me!"

☯ *Love Light: Going Along for the Ride*

Very few people hitchhike on the roads these days because it is dangerous. Drivers don't trust strangers on the street and vice versa. But we can "hitchhike" spiritually on life's highway and have a safe, good time in the process.

I once saw an incredibly tiny boat that could barely fit one man sitting down. The plaque in the museum said that it was the smallest craft ever to cross the Atlantic Ocean. When the explorer was asked why it was so small, he answered: "It's simple. A small craft bobs on top of the water when storms come or things get choppy. The heavier the vessel, the more likely it is to capsize or sink."

Many of us try to sail through life in the mental and spiritual equivalents of the *Titanic*. We think we have safe, sturdy, unsink-able ships until life puts an iceberg in our path. In the end, we may not have enough rowboats and lifeboats to survive the disaster, and we are sunk.

I'm not recommending that you do what Dexter did, but rather think about Dexter's mindset as he went on his adventure. He was happy, relaxed, and open to his own inner visions. We all have these, but few of us pay attention. I believe that God gives us these to lead and reassure us, but we rarely respond. Dexter did and was perfectly content to wait for things to unfold as he had experienced them with his inner eye.

You can, too. Close your eyes and let a vision of happiness arise from your heart. See yourself as safe, free, happy. If you see no pictures, listen for sounds, smells, tastes, or textures. These, too, are physical reassurances that something wonderful is about to happen.

Go forth in confidence. Wonders are waiting for you.

Back in a Flash

The wonder of a sign that everything's all right

*O*f all the challenges we face in life, few are more emotionally and spiritually trying than facing a loved one's suicide. There are countless unanswered questions, not only of what could have been done differently here on earth to prevent the tragedy, but of what the hosts of heaven must be thinking now.

If a sudden death of any kind is unsettling, suicide is even more so. Never is the need for reassurance or personal peace greater or harder to find. But once in a great while, in the midst of heavy despair and grief, something wonderful happens to light the way and suggest that everything will be all right.

RODNEY WAS CAROL'S OLDER BROTHER. He was also her best friend and confidant. "Rodney was a very compassionate man with a deep caring for people less fortunate than himself," Carol says. Rodney was always there for Carol and she for him, particularly in the fifteen months after his separation and divorce. Rodney became depressed, and even medication didn't seem to help. When Carol called her brother on a Friday night in April 1992, she sensed that something was terribly wrong, even though Rodney said nothing unusual. "Our last words to one another were 'I love you!' " she remembers. Little did she know it would be the final time she would speak to him.

She called him again on Saturday night and left a cheerful message on his answering machine, assuming he was out for the evening. When she called on Sunday morning and got his machine again, she hung up and called their parents. "Have you seen Rodney?" she asked. "I was wondering if he had mentioned plans to leave town for the weekend." They replied that Rodney had taken them to dinner the previous Wednesday but hadn't said anything about going anywhere over the weekend.

Carol called Rodney again. When he didn't answer, she quickly hopped in her car and drove over to his house. She was relieved to see his truck in the driveway as she approached but surprised to find that the engine was cold when she touched it. It was obvious that he had not just returned.

Worried, she knocked on the door. No answer. She rang the bell. Nothing. She called out his name. No response. She opened the door with the spare key Rodney had given her and walked all through the downstairs of the house, calling his name. Still no answer.

She went upstairs. Outside his bedroom, she noticed feet under the covers of his bed. It was Rodney. His eyes were open, but he had blood running from his nose and mouth. She ran over to him, but then noticed he was still holding a pistol in his right hand.

"Why, Rodney? Why?" Carol wailed. She nervously checked

his pulse, even though she knew that her darling brother was gone.

Carol grabbed the phone and dialed 911. She could barely speak but somehow managed to convey that her brother had shot himself and she believed he was dead. The operator asked the address, and Carol suddenly went blank. She couldn't remember it! Fortunately, the emergency system was able to locate the address, and Carol confirmed that, yes, it was correct.

When the police officer arrived, Carol went downstairs to let him in. She never returned to her brother's bedroom again. The emergency medical technicians arrived next, bringing their life-support equipment, but there was no need. Fortunately, they had brought a minister with them, because, as Carol says, "I sure did need one at that point. I was in shock and could barely breathe."

Carol needed air and finally went outside. When she did, something wonderful happened. The day was sunny and clear, with a brilliant blue sky dotted with a few puffy white clouds. But when Carol turned her face toward heaven, she saw two unmistakable flashes of lightning. "I was the only one outside at the time," she remembers. "But I knew I was watching Rodney's soul entering heaven. When I found Rodney, his Bible was nearby. He obviously was praying before he took his life. The look on his face was so full of peace and awe that I just knew he had seen the light of the Lord."

One month later, Carol was attending her niece's college graduation in another state. Sleep had not come easily to her in the weeks following Rodney's death, and now she lay in bed, wide awake. Then another wonderful thing happened. "I saw white lights come towards me that formed Rodney's face!" she exclaims. "He was smiling, and I knew then that he was at peace and that I didn't need to worry about him anymore."

Now, whenever Carol hears one of Rodney's favorite songs

or sees a blue sky dotted with clouds, she talks to her brother. "When I do, I always feel a surge of electricity travel from my head to my toes," she says, "and I know that Rodney is communicating with me. All I have to do is acknowledge his presence with the words 'I love you!'"

"I don't believe that God forgives only those with physical pain," she says. "Sometimes those with mental pain and anguish are hurting even more. That pain can't be seen, but people close to them can feel it. Rodney was a blessing given by God, and I believe God wanted him back so he could go on to do more wonderful, blessed things."

⑨ Love Light: Letting Love Enter

The two wonders that Carol experienced—the twin flashes of lightning and the appearance of Rodney's face—happened when her defenses were down. She was shocked and weary beyond belief. Wonders often enter when we are at our most vulnerable emotionally and spiritually because we have no resistance to them. Unfortunately, this may also be the time that we are least aware that they are happening. But Carol looked up and opened her eyes, and there were the wonders, reassuring her at the time she needed it most.

If you have experienced a tragedy in your life, you, too, might be in great need of a wondrous sign of reassurance. You might be able to receive one in either of two ways. One is to ask, simply and purely, before you go to bed at night. It will likely appear in a dream or as something you see or hear when you awaken. Be patient if it doesn't happen the first night. If you do not fully believe in signs or feel you might be frightened by the appearance of one, it will not show up until you are ready.

The second way is to sit quietly in either meditation or prayer. For the former, concentrate on watching your breath rise and fall. If thoughts come up, acknowledge them, but dismiss them quickly and go back to your breathing. Soon you will find yourself relaxed, and wonders can enter. If you choose the path of prayer, try concentrating on the attributes of God rather than on the tragedy. Again, if angry or contradictory thoughts arise, acknowledge and dismiss them quickly. Just think about love, grace, mercy, wisdom, and loving-kindness.

If you find that neither of these ideas works for you or if they make you even more resistant to the idea of wonder, you may want to seek the alternative course of professional counseling to help you achieve peace. Sometimes the angels we need are right here on earth to guide, reassure, and open us. Either way, the improvement in the way you see yourself and the situation will be wonderful.

On Eagles' Wings

The wonder of true dedication

*I*t's easy to have a dream; much harder to make it come true. Although the idea of facing a tremendous challenge seems heroic, the fact is that it's more human to want an easy reward than one that uses our sweat, blood, and money. But sometimes a dream is so luminous that the bumps in the road can hardly be felt. The light at the end of the tunnel shines so brightly that darkness and the fear it brings are all but eliminated. If we can see ourselves radiant and alive at the end of our journey before we even take the first step, wonderful things can happen.

EVERYONE WHO HAD EVER worked with Duane called him "The Eagle" for his keen eye, penetrating insights, and ability to communicate a vision. He was humble about the comparison but liked it because, to him, eagles symbolized freedom, beauty, family loyalty, and discovery.

Duane decided to strike out on his own as a consultant, but the vision for his business was anything but eagle-eyed. For more than six years, he took whatever work came his way, doing the best job he could but not feeling truly passionate about it.

As time went on, he became more and more restless. He wanted to embrace a single purpose and throw everything he had into it, but it wasn't clear what that passion could be. Eventually, he found himself especially drawn to news about the farm economy, even though most of it was full of dire predictions. He liked talking to farmers, since he had grown up on a farm and loved the close familial and community life it provided. But it was obvious that change was needed. He saw fingers of blame pointing in all directions, particularly toward those in government or politics. He learned about the isolation of independent farmers. Many families who had been on the land for generations were forced to quit, leaving them emotionally and financially adrift. "It was an opportunity to be of service," he says, "and I felt I could have a passion for it." So one day, The Eagle decided he would commit himself completely to business activities that would link small-town farmers with profitable opportunities.

The road to success was not even a trail when Duane began. No one believed that the market held any promise for small producers, so Duane was on his own. Armed with nothing but an insatiable desire, he started making calls. "I had to qualify myself to be able to talk about this knowledgeably," he said. "There were a lot of other people who knew a lot about different parts of it, although no one person seemed to understand or know about the full spectrum of things. I decided to be that person."

Duane made a lot of appointments and put thousands of miles on his car as he traveled to talk to people in the know. He visited government offices of agriculture and economic development. He attended countless regional council meetings as an observer. He spent time at area agricultural colleges. He met with farmers, cooperatives, and bankers. "Each contact reinforced the other," Duane said. "It was like adding clay to clay, bringing each small piece together to contribute to the larger vision."

As Duane sought to learn how to make money for farmers, he gave up his own income. For months, all of his time and traveling was on his own dime. Nothing was reimbursed, and initially no consulting contracts were in sight. He maxed out his credit cards and wore out his tires. But he pressed on, fed by the belief that what he was doing was going to work out well for everyone in the end.

Besides the money, Duane faced a few other humbling incidents along the way. More than once he found himself in situations in which he felt, "You have so much more to learn." He didn't know enough about some of the new crops and farm programs. Eventually, he learned to listen first and echo back what he was being told as opposed to trying to convince those with experience in the industry to change their minds. "When they heard their words coming from my mouth, they were able to say, 'Yes, that's right.' That was the start."

Although he was gaining contacts and knowledge, the experts continued to doubt his vision of linking small-town farmers directly with profitable opportunities. Still, he pressed on, undaunted. "I never changed direction, even if someone didn't see my vision clearly," he says. "I never doubted what needed to be done. I simply invited each person to join me in reaching the vision and let each one decide his or her own level of commitment. Whatever they wanted or were able to do was fine with me."

Six months into his effort, Duane was talking to several bureaucrats about his vision. He listened closely as they explained their own frustrations with the processes and limited resources they were forced to use. Duane applied his fresh perspective to what they already believed. And when he did, at last something wonderful happened.

"One of the people stopped the conversation, looked at me, and said, 'What do we need to do to help this eagle soar?'" Duane remembers. "Maybe they finally saw the possibility of these opportunities actually being created, or maybe they just wanted to share my passion. People love to be part of something truly positive. But either way, they threw themselves wholeheartedly behind what I was trying to do." He was surprised. They had no idea of the nickname given to him twenty years earlier by people in another industry.

Before long, Duane was making complex deals with unheard-of speed and accuracy and getting paid well for his expertise and hard work. He bought processing plants for producers, helped launch cooperatives, and filled abandoned property in small towns with viable businesses. Today, he continues to strengthen what he calls his "three-legged stool": opportunity, financing, and knowledge for small-town producers. He has a waiting list of potential clients, and he's happy.

"I'm home," he says. "This is the most peaceful place I've ever been from a work standpoint. It's energizing, rewarding, and joyful." As he's quick to tell you, it's a wonderful place to be.

☉ *Love Light: Taking the Leap*

In order for wonderful things to start happening for Duane, he had to do two things. First, he had to have a clear vision of what he wanted. Once he knew why he wanted to help small farm producers, he was able to enhance his passion for the challenge. He did not know how he was going to do it, only that somehow, some way, he would.

The second thing he had to do was take a leap of faith. In the many months when he was networking and learning, Duane had little or no income. Fortunately, he had a hard-working spouse who was still drawing a salary, but financially it was a trying time. It is very difficult not to be obsessed with money or even potential earnings at times like these. Whenever fear or doubt arose, Duane would push them aside and just keep going on his mission. He never thought about how much money he could earn, because no one had ever done what he was trying to do. So his plan was not about the money, at least not for himself. Rather, it was about people, other people, and how his visions could secure their well-being, growth, and peace of mind. By keeping that focus, he ended up with a stream of work and income that suited him nicely.

You can do the same. If you have a vision of how life could be made better for others, act on it. Do whatever you must to begin, and never look back, for doubt and fear will hang in your shadow for a long time. Similarly, do not look too far into the future, for if the horizon seems too distant, you may tire before you reach it.

Instead, look around you and ask, "Who will be served by this?" The answer is right where you are. Respond to the best of your ability—nothing more, nothing less. Don't worry about what you do not know. You will learn it or find someone who does. Just keep going. Remember to stop and rest along the way to review exactly how far you have come. Celebrate every accomplishment, for when you do, you open the stream to a lifetime of wonder.

The Comeback

The wonder of living to reach a special moment

We all have moments in life we dream about: our first kiss, our high school graduation, our wedding day, and so on. Once these milestones are achieved, we live for lesser experiences — a vacation, for instance, or a new car. For those who have children or grandchildren, the cycle of life begins anew. We look forward to seeing them reach their milestones . . . if our health allows it. When physical challenges enter, wonders often disappear as we concentrate on managing the illness or disability. Ironically, wonders also can reappear, especially if there is a moment of relief or pause where the radiance of life shines through. When this happens, it's wonderful.

"I'VE GOT TO SEE JESSICA GROW UP," Beth said when she learned she had Hodgkin's disease, a form of cancer. "That was my goal.

Jessica had just started first grade. And I knew that as long as I stayed focused on being there for her, I could get through it."

Beth had actually been sick for almost two years before she was correctly diagnosed. "I went to doctors, but nobody knew what was wrong with me," she said. "One day, I was making stuffed cabbage for Rosh Hashanah, and I said to one of my friends, 'Feel this.' There was a huge lump on my neck."

After that, Beth began a grueling protocol of chemotherapy. She almost died from septic shock when one of the chemo lines became infected, but she hung on, determined to live to see her daughter grow up.

Beth's treatments ended two years later and her health seemed to stabilize. Time passed, and soon both Beth and Jessica were approaching milestones. Beth was turning forty in the fall, and Jessica, at age thirteen, was preparing for her Bat Mitzvah, a ceremony that symbolizes entering religious adulthood in the Jewish community. In the background of those two happy occasions was one that no one in the family wanted to jinx: September would also represent Beth's fifth year of being disease-free, which meant her doctors considered her original cancer to no longer be a threat to her.

The morning of Jessica's Bat Mitzvah was perfect. The sky was sapphire blue, the air New England tangy with the scents, smells, and sounds of early autumn. Beth and Jessica both wore white dresses and looked like angels. Beth's family had gathered from all across the country to share the first real celebration since Beth had been sick. "It touched my heart that so much of my extended family was there," she said, "including relatives who normally would not come up to Vermont. I loved the fact that we were all together."

Beth, her husband, Jon, and Jessica had written the prayer

service especially for the occasion. In addition to the traditional prayers, they added special readings and poems that celebrated life. Each one was presented by a special person in Jessica's life. It was a way of saying, "Each life matters, and we're glad you are here."

As the ceremony ended, something wonderful happened. Normally, a blessing is said, a song is sung, and the service ends with hugs and handshakes all around. But when Jessica finished, someone started applauding. They kept on until everyone was on their feet, clapping.

Beth and Jon stood up and went up into the pulpit to hug and stand beside their daughter. Beth had made it. Jessica had made it. The family had made it through. Life had won.

There wasn't a dry eye in the sanctuary as the final hymn was sung. Beth, Jessica, and Jon were going forward with their lives. One of the poems they'd selected told everyone so. It was Robert Frost's "Stopping By the Woods on a Snowy Evening," which ends with these words:

"But I have promises to keep,
And miles to go before I sleep,
And miles to go before I sleep."

"It was an emotional day," Jon says. "We were feeling very fortunate and very proud."

"There was a completion that day," Beth says. "We succeeded, and it was time to keep moving and keep enjoying life."

✸ *Love Light: 1,440 Minutes*

I like to play a game with the people in my workshops. I say, "I have fourteen hundred and forty dollars for each one of you in this room, but there's a catch. You have twenty-four hours to spend it. If you do, it's yours to keep. If you don't, you have to give me back whatever you don't spend. How many of you could do that?"

Invariably, every hand in the room shoots up. "Good," I then say. "And tomorrow, we play the same game with the same rules. How many of you could do it a second time?" Again, no one has ever failed to mentally spend the money. I go on to say that we will play this forever until they have all they want and everyone becomes a rich philanthropist. When they start laughing, I say, "Well, each one of us receives fourteen hundred and forty minutes every day. You can spend them on things you want, or you can waste them and give them back to God unused. Which will it be?"

Beth, Jon, and Jessica know how they would answer. The question is: Do you? How many wonderful minutes of your life have you thrown or given away or ignored? Milestones are great, but we only enjoy so many in our lifetimes.

Starting today, think about challenges you have overcome, including those you may be facing right now. Pause and reflect. Give yourself a pat on the back or a sip of champagne for every one. If you want wonderful things to happen in your life, begin by noting those that already have happened. You may have experienced more than you think.

Once you have reviewed your treasures, put them away in your heart. Pick yourself up, face the future, and take another first step. Don't be afraid. The rewards awaiting you are wonderful.

Go, Babies, Go!

The wonder of communicating with animals

"*Y*ou don't understand!" we scream with rage when someone does not respond to our needs or wishes. This is especially bad with people who not only speak our language but supposedly care about us. What wonderful things might happen if we could communicate telepathically, empathetically, through feeling only? What if we could warn one another of danger long before it happens? Would the world seem kinder, safer, more secure for everyone?

Although we think that children's language skills are especially primitive, I have read many books that say this is not so. Children, because of their innocence, are able to communicate with life forms adults cannot. There are many anecdotal stories about children and their guardian angels and even more about their ability to "talk to the animals," as Dr. Doolittle would say. They often do this without worrying about the limitations of language, simply by allowing their hearts to speak. When they do, wonderful things can happen.

"THE BULLDOZER IS COMING TOMORROW," Steve said at dinner. "And then we kiss that old garage good-bye."

I was glad to hear it. The garage was detached from our 115-year-old house, and it was falling down. The doors were so warped they wouldn't close half the time. The roof was leaking and the gutters were rotted. Every time we put one of our cars inside, we wondered if we would find it buried beneath rubble in the morning. "A strong wind would do it," I said. "But I'll be just as glad to have it over and done with quickly. It'll be great to have a new garage that actually does what it's supposed to."

Our eight-year-old daughter, Amanda, was listening. "Will the raccoons live in the new garage?" she asked naively.

We hoped not. We found evidence of raccoons rummaging through our garbage cans and saw them running on the roof of the garage but had no proof that they had actually taken up residence. Or, more accurately, we didn't care to find out. The last thing either Steve or I needed was to be more afraid to set foot in that shaky place. The idea of a raccoon jumping down and landing on our heads from the rafters was just too much.

For months, we avoided the issue. Our two daughters, however, did not. We would often find them in the playroom, peeking out the little peephole window as soon as it got dark outside. Although we never saw anything, they told us tales about a mama, papa, and three baby raccoons appearing and disappearing in the walls of the garage. We made up bedtime stories about it and tried to keep it a fantasy.

The story would come to a crashing end—literally—when

the contractor knocked the building down to make way for the new structure. We didn't think the girls needed to be prepared for this, but they had other ideas. They didn't need to be warned; they wanted to warn the raccoon family. At their insistence, we took a flashlight and went out into the yard to "have a talk" with our furry guests.

We shined the light onto a hole in the guttering that the girls pointed out. "Raccoons!" Amanda called. "We have to tell you something." Lo and behold, five sets of eyes appeared in the horizontal crack. I shivered, even though it was a warm night in June.

"A bulldozer is coming!" our baby called. "You have to get out!"

"Go to the river," the elder chimed in. "You'll be safe there, and there's plenty of food."

The raccoons made no sound and did not come out from their hiding place. "Okay, girls, you told them. Now let's go to bed," I said. After we went in the house, we all looked out the playroom window and saw all five walking across the garage roof to the alley.

The next morning when the bulldozer arrived, we stopped the contractor before he drove up the tiny hill to the garage. "There are raccoons in there," we warned, handing him a baseball bat. "Since you're destroying their habitat, they may attack. You might need this."

He nodded, rolled down his sleeves, and took the bat. He revved the engine a few times in warning, then hurtled forward. The garage came down with a thunderous crash. But then something wonderful happened. No raccoons came running out of the debris. As he began hauling away the remains of the structure, we looked for evidence of five dead raccoons. But even after the last board and nail were picked up, there wasn't any.

"See? They understood us," Amanda said smugly at dinner that night.

"They got away, safe and sound," Erica agreed.

"I guess they went to the river," Steve said.

"Or found a good garbage can or two to hide in," I suggested, thinking that I'd let someone else take out the garbage for the time being.

But for now, one thing was certain: The raccoons had escaped unharmed. And that was wonderful.

❤ Love Light: Talk to the Animals

Dr. Doolittle could do it. So could Cinderella. If you have a pet, you may do it, too. Talking to animals. Their sounds are foreign to us (and ours to them), but the one thing both species understand is the language of love. Although we will never know if it was just dumb luck that saved the raccoons' lives that day, our girls were completely convinced it was their warnings that made the difference.

Since I travel often in rural areas, I decided to try an experiment. When I get on the road, I say, "Okay, deer, squirrels, skunks, gophers, and raccoons. There's plenty of room out here for all of us. Please cross the road well ahead of me or after I'm gone." So far, so good. In twenty-three years, I have had all nature of beasts cross my path, but always at a distance.

You might want to try the same trick. Our minds are very powerful tools, and every thought that carries a strong emotion actually goes out from us like a radar beam to find its receiver. Try testing this wondrous power. Make a request from the heart to the birds, the butterflies, or your cat. Close your eyes and see them nodding in understanding. If this is too awkward for you, ask a small child to do it for you. Something wonderful always happens when you do.

Pain, Pain, Go Away

The healing wonder of lightening up

*W*hen Norman Cousins was diagnosed with a fatal illness, he changed his perspective by turning his attention away from his disease and toward videos and other things that made him laugh. The result was wonderful: He recovered fully and went on to live many more happy, productive years, which he documented in his famous book, *Anatomy of an Illness*.

When we hurt, it's easy to take our pain and resulting situation seriously. Although we want to heal quickly, we focus on what is bothering or worrying us, which usually just makes us feel worse. That's where other people come in. For when someone brings us hope or happiness in the midst of suffering, wonderful things happen.

LUIGI HURT. At age fifty-five, he suffered from heart problems that led to a quadruple bypass. Although he was a talented and accomplished actor, comedy writer, and director, the event left him feeling depressed and discouraged.

However, his wife, Ann, was not defeated by the situation. An actress, Ann loved to play and pretend. For almost two decades, she had performed a mixture of her own characters and Mother Goose at public libraries, schools, bookstores, festivals, museums, and parties. Ann knew the powers of joy and fun. So as she was driving Luigi home from the hospital, Ann suggested they stop at the boat basin at the foot of the Palisades, in northern New Jersey, to relax and look at the river for a while.

As Luigi sat and stared at the water, Ann did something wonderful. "Hey, diddle diddle! Luigi and his fiddle. His heart jumped over the moon!" she sang. Then she began to dance around her husband. "Pick yourself up, dust yourself off, and start all over again!"

Her play was magnetic to some children who were passing by, and Ann immediately drew them into her act. Although Luigi was still in pain, he could not help but move around a bit himself. As he did, he started to feel better.

The couple headed home, but Ann kept up with her nursery rhyme "medicine." As Luigi fell asleep that night, she sang, "Pain, pain, go away! Luigi wants to play today. Don't come back another day. Just hurry on your way." Then she sang "The Itsy Bitsy Spider" as she tenderly rubbed her husband's chest with aloe.

Luigi thought his wife's playfulness was silly, but he had to admit that he felt better when she did it. He started thinking about his wife's positive attitude and the value her humor had on his well-being.

"Her Mother Goose rhymes tapped the child in me," he says. "I was far too serious about my illness. I knew I needed to pull back to the basics, or my life would be over."

He thought back to his mother, who lay dying in the hospital the year before. When he went to visit, he took a book by Dante to read to her, one of his mother's favorite authors. But as he started voicing some of the dark passages, his mother protested. "Please, no!" It happened that Luigi had a book of Mother Goose stories with him because Ann had asked him to write a script for a new program she wanted to do. So he opened it and started reading rhymes to his mother. When he got to "There was an old woman who lived in a shoe," his mother laughed and said, "Not Pop's shoe!" "My mother wanted to go out thinking light thoughts, not something dark," Luigi says. "Mother Goose revived her for a moment or two."

Luigi's perspective changed in wonderful ways as he recovered. "Maybe we get away from the things of our youth too soon," he says. "We get too serious, and that hurts us. The Chinese have a story that says we must be like bamboo. Bamboo waves in the wind. If it remained stiff, the wind would crack it. But if we are like the bamboo, absorbing the force of the wind, we can get back to our normal positions. You need to know how to give and take, weave and bend when life blows strong winds in your direction. In time, I began to understand that is what Mother Goose is really all about."

Before long, Luigi was inspired to direct again. He chose William Inge's *Bus Stop*, which was performed at New Jersey's Teaneck New Theatre. "It's a play about the human need for love, which mostly escapes the majority of people," Luigi says. "Inge is really saying, 'Life ain't so grand.' " Then he laughs. "Without Mother Goose."

Luigi is now "retired," although he frequently appears with his wife at her many performances. "I play a snare drum to punctuate my wife's stories," he explains. "I'm the *ba-ba-da-boom!* guy." Luigi also enchants the children by becoming one of the key characters in Ann's interactive stories. He likes to keep the kids guessing. "I play a wise old woman," he says with a laugh. "The kids come to me to get ideas for what the main character can do next. I'm always 'sleeping,' and they have to wake me up. Sometimes I tear off my kerchief or make silly grins with my big 'buck' teeth. For our next performances, I may put on a 'bald' wig. So when the kerchief comes off, they'll really be surprised!" Luigi looks forward to participating in Ann's performances because the fun and laughter make him feel better and better.

Luigi has written a book called *Homecrest Ave.: Silhouettes of an Accidental Family*. The final chapter, "Ain't Life Grand," features a story about his widowed father, who had a love affair at age ninety-three. Luigi is also looking forward to the fun and adventure of many more wonderful years.

Luigi says his new perspective didn't happen overnight. "It's taken years," he admits. "I asked myself, 'Why am I crippling myself before my time?' You can't get better going through life looking through a rearview mirror. I learned how to control my excitability. Ann once said to me, 'Every time someone puts a grenade on the table, you don't have to pick it up.' And she's right."

Luigi admits that Ann's attitude and perspective have made life a lot more wonderful for him. "What I loved about Ann from the beginning is that when she wakes up, she's smiling." These days, Luigi spends more time smiling, too.

♥ *Love Light: Funny Thing!*

We human beings tend to take ourselves and our own lives too seriously. We are obsessed with work, obligations, and a need for recognition. It's easy to become so narrowly focused that we forget to have fun, especially the kind that costs little or nothing.

To make something wonderful happen, try finding something to laugh about. Try not to make your laughter come at someone else's expense. Rather, follow Norman Cousins's lead and rent comedy videos, or try Ann's idea of using nursery rhymes in playful new ways. You can get on the Internet and find dozens of sites with free jokes or go shopping for silly stuff in the local mall. Best of all, call a friend, get together, and laugh away an afternoon.

It's actually impossible to feel bad when you're smiling. If you don't believe this, put on a grin from ear to ear and say out loud, "I feel bad. I really do!" You will likely crack up with laughter, not only because it seems ridiculous to be smiling when you say something like that, but because smiles release chemicals in our bloodstreams that make us feel good.

And while you're feeling good, expect some of the trouble in your life to fade just a bit. Because when we are feeling positive, bad things have a hard time sticking, and good things have a chance to enter. I once advised a real estate agent who'd gone six months without a single sale. "I have to work this weekend!" he insisted. "I have to make dozens of calls!" Instead, I suggested that he forget the work and go to his brother's house, where he was invited to swim and play with his nephews. Finally, he agreed to go and had a wonderful time. When he got home, there was not one, but two potential sales waiting on his answering machine.

So laugh. Life is wonderful if you want it to be.

Heavenly Music

The wonder of connecting with joy

As you've seen from the stories in this book, sometimes it feels as though all the cosmic tumblers just click into place and the locked door to happiness that we've been pushing against swings open without any effort at all. Although it looks effortless, it's actually very difficult for most people, most of the time, because our egos get in the way of our souls' natural ability to attract what is good for it. In this book, you've seen wonders come when pain and trouble have worn people down. But it also comes when we are weary from happiness, totally content with the moment at hand. When we want or need nothing, wonders happen.

MY DREAM HAD COME TRUE: I was in New York City promoting my first "big" book, *The Ten Gifts*. I couldn't have been any happier about it. My whole extended family and many old friends were on hand during a launch party, and we enjoyed an evening that was full of laughs, hugs, and huge quantities of catching up. Everyone was happy and excited, but none more so than I.

My publicist had suggested that we "go for it" while I was in town, so I willingly said yes to back-to-back interviews during the first twenty-four hours. I had been up since 3:00 A.M. because only the red-eye flight would deliver me, my husband, and our two daughters to the East Coast in time for the first festivities. The party was over at about 9:00 P.M., at which point our daughters headed back to the suburbs with my parents, and my brother dropped Steve and me off at the hotel to get some dinner and rest.

The latter was short-lived for me, however, because I had to be at a radio station for an all-night talk show at midnight. By 4:00 A.M., the host and I were having a ball on the air, but I told him I had to go rest again, since I had to be on a train to Westchester at 7:00 A.M. I laid down for about an hour before I got up again, showered, and headed for the train station.

I was running on pure adrenaline, but I didn't care. I loved everything about what was happening—the people, the places, the excitement, the potential. All I wanted was more. But after thirty-plus hours with basically no sleep, I needed some downtime. I returned to my hotel late in the morning, lay down, and promptly fell into some heavy zzzzzzzs.

My hotel was directly across from Lincoln Center, the world-renowned concert hall on the west side of Manhattan. Some of the best music and dance performances in the world are presented there. As I was growing up, I attended quite a few, since I am orig-inally from New Jersey. This trip, however, there was no time for me to attend a performance. But as I lay on my bed, something wonderful happened.

I heard music. It was the most beautiful music I had ever

heard in my life. It sounded like a boys' choir, but it was more than that. The sound was so rich and full that there had to be thousands of singers, and I began to wonder which one of Lincoln Center's stages would be big enough for that. It sounded like a spiritual group. They were singing about joy, joy, and more joy. When did Lincoln Center start featuring such music? I wondered.

Then I stopped wondering and just let the music flood my senses. I felt like I was floating on a sea of beauty, bobbing up and down with the swells in the melody. I didn't hear the music so much as feel it in every fiber of my being. It felt so good that I didn't want it to stop. And, wonderfully, it didn't. There didn't seem to be a beginning or an end to the song—it just went on and on and on. If there was an audience, they were silent. There was no pause nor any applause. Just an unending sense of beauty, love, and peace.

The sound was so close that I felt like I was in an auditorium with it. Where was this concert being held, anyway—outdoors? Or did Lincoln Center now have loudspeakers on the outside of its buildings to broadcast the performances to passersby? I knew I wasn't sleeping, but I hadn't yet opened my eyes. I was almost afraid to. I wanted to continue enjoying the concert from the comfort of my bed.

I opened my eyes for an instant and glanced at the clock. It was 12:30 P.M. "Lincoln Center would never have a concert at this hour," I thought. I got up and looked out the window. It was quiet across the street. There was no choir in the courtyard, no loudspeakers. The only sound I heard was that of traffic—horns honking, brakes squealing, tires whizzing down the city streets. I wondered why I had not heard them just moments before.

I sat down to try to come to grips with what had happened. Had I been dreaming? No, I was too aware of my surroundings for that. Was it just my imagination? I had never heard or experienced anything like it before, so I found it hard to believe I had made it up. "What was that?" I asked God.

Instantly, I was reminded of a story in one of Sophy Burnham's angel books about a man who lived alone in rural West Virginia. He, too, heard a choir, which he thought was coming from the valley below him. One day, he and his nephew were rocking on the front porch of his house when he asked the younger man what he thought of the music. "What music, uncle?" the nephew answered. "I don't hear anything."

When his nephew left, the old man stood up and called out, "Who's thar?" And the answer came back in his own *patois*: "*This y'er's heaven. C'aint neverbody hear it.*" I knew then that in my happy, relaxed, and satisfied state of mind, I had heard heaven. I just knew it. And I had to giggle, because I've always loved to sing. If someday I, too, end up in that choir, that would be wonderful.

❀ *Love Light: Let Heaven and Nature Sing!*

I had not planned to hear a heavenly choir that day. My guess is that if I had, I wouldn't have heard it. The reason it happened, I believe, is because I was totally nonresistant to it. I was physically exhausted and emotionally satisfied when I fell onto the bed that day. I felt complete—there was nothing I wanted or needed. How many wonders do we miss because we are too focused on our earthly needs?

Now, just for fun, try to tune in to the "music" of the life around you. It's a very different perspective for most of us because all too often we feel we are simply bombarded by noise. But what if underneath the noise, beyond the din, there is a sweet symphony? What if life has been singing to you for years, waiting for you to join in?

Scientists tell us that every object and life form does, indeed, have its own sound vibration. Including you. Whether you are speaking, singing, or silent, you emit vibrations that come from the continuous action of the atoms and molecules that comprise your physical form. You can't hear it, but you can feel it, especially when you are around others. We say that people have "good vibrations" or "bad vibrations," and we know how these affect us when we are near them. The same is true in reverse. You are constantly giving off energy to the people, animals, and plant life around you.

If you want to try something wonderful, listen for this invisible "music." It's in everyone and everything. Feel it with your heart rather than trying to tune in your ears. Try to harmonize your thoughts with what you sense.

If that seems too esoteric for you, listen to the actual symphony of life: Birds singing. Leaves whispering in a summer breeze. Tires making contact with a concrete highway. The mainframe motor of a computer. Everything has a nature of some kind, its own unique note. If you tune in, you will hear it, feel it, know it. Try humming with it. When you do, your sense of connection to the life around you grows. And that's wonderful.

"They Shall Walk and Not Faint"

The wonder of knowing everything will be all right

There is, unfortunately, no such thing as a life without tragedy. The question is not merely, "How do we cope?" but "What have we learned?" For sometimes, deep within the darkness, there is the light of perfect peace. In spite of current circumstances, we realize that all is truly well and life will go on. The comfort of that is, indeed, wonderful.

ONE OF DENNIS'S FAVORITE VERSES of scripture was Isaiah 40:31: "Those who wait for the Lord shall renew their strength. They shall mount up with wings like eagles. They shall run and not be weary. They shall walk and not faint." It hung on the wall of his office as a piece of cross-stitch made by his mother, and he had it programmed into his computer in Saudi Arabia as a screen saver. The verse was firmly planted in his mind and his heart, which was a good thing, because on the night of June 25, 1996, it was put to the test in a way Dennis never could have imagined.

Dennis was serving overseas as the senior chaplain for the U.S. Air Force 4404th Wing (Provisional) in Dhahran. His tour had been "both challenging and richly satisfying," he says, but it was time to go home. He was one day away from welcoming the air force chaplain who would replace him and one week from returning to his family and home base in Las Vegas, Nevada.

"I was feeling peaceful with a growing excitement as I entered that final week," Dennis said. By 10 P.M. that Tuesday, he headed for the chaplain's suite to get a good night's rest.

But it was not to be. "I heard a loud boom, a blast wave, and the sound of shattered glass flying everywhere," he says. "There was sudden darkness and then a short-lived, deathly silence." Miraculously, both Dennis and another chaplain were uninjured, so they headed out immediately, trying to find the point of greatest human need.

It didn't take long to find out what had happened: Terrorists had made good on their threat to harm Americans. A large truck bomb had caused nineteen deaths and hundreds of injuries.

"The adrenaline flow and divine strength took over," Dennis said. He and the other chaplain and a chaplain support specialist all went directly to the air force and army clinics in Khobar Towers, where the injured were being brought. As the medical triage took place, they did a spiritual triage. "I was called on twice to pray over people who had died," Dennis recalls. For both the victims and the rescue workers, he offered prayers and words of support and comfort as he helped bear litters and pass out bottled water.

"Feelings of hopelessness and despair could have ruled the day, given the enormity of this disaster," Dennis says. But in the midst of tragedy, something wonderful happened. "The bomb blast had taken place in the dark of night. As dawn broke, I went to the doorway and just stood there, watching the light. Behind me, people were doing their best to prepare the dead for transport to the United States. But before me there was light; and even with the broken bodies, broken spirits, and the night of grim work with the mortuary affairs team, I had an inexplicable feeling of peace," he explains. "I call it an inward assurance that we were being propelled and sustained through this experience by a power of infinite compassion and love that was far greater than ourselves."

On the morning of June 28, Dennis and his staff were responsible for leading memorial services for the victims of the bombing. The congregation of almost 500 people included other chaplains who had been sent in by the various branches of the U.S. and British armed forces and many international journalists. Normally, Dennis would have taken time to write out his homily on his computer. But another bomb scare forced him to evacuate again. All he could do was "scribble notes on three little pieces of paper, a far cry from my normal mode of message preparation, which would have been a reasonably full manuscript," he remembers.

But once again, something wonderful happened. "I felt a strange and undeniable sense, a peacefulness, that things would be okay," he says. "I had a strong sense of the divine and truly felt that God was in control." One of Dennis's fellow eulogists was a squadron commander who had narrowly escaped death himself. When the blast occurred, the commander's roommate had been killed instantly, less than ten feet away from him. A dividing wall saved his life. He had lost five members of his unit and was on crutches himself. Dennis had no idea what the commander would say when it came his turn to speak. He was surprised when the commander chose the very quote from Isaiah that hung on Dennis's wall.

Dennis struggled with his own peaks and valleys of grief and guilt at not being injured as the week wore on. " 'Why them and not me?' is a question I can't answer," Dennis says. "Catastrophic events remind me of how fragile life is and what a tremendous gift it is."

In the end, he made it. "When the bomb blew, life and our responsibilities as chaplains went to warp speed," he says. "I looked to the kind of strength I believe God promised in the words of Isaiah — 'to run and not be weary.' And the bottom line is that I made it through an incredible week. I'm here to tell you that my prayer for that kind of strength was answered. Indeed, I'm sure it was the prayer uttered by many of the people most impacted by this nightmare, especially the families and closest friends of the victims, whose trauma and loss far exceeds anything I experienced."

Reflecting back, Dennis adds: "I believe God's promise to Joshua is also made to us, to 'be strong and courageous and neither frightened nor dismayed, for the Lord your God is with you wherever you go.' It's true whether we're dealing with a personal crisis or a senseless act of violence with tragic consequences."

⊛ *Love Light: Wonder-full Words*

Dennis says that the words of Isaiah are very special to his family and have seen them through many life challenges. Perhaps you, too, have a chapter or verse from the Bible, the Torah, or Koran that resonates with your soul. If so, that is what I like to call your "Wonderful!" prayer.

If you are not religious, you may use another quote or stated value as your personal guiding light. If you are spiritually creative, perhaps you have even written one for yourself.

But if you don't have one, today is a good day to find wonder-*full* words that make you feel safe, calm, and confident. So read. Ask. Listen—to God, to the still small voice within your own heart, or to the people around you, who often act as messengers just when we need it most.

Make those words yours. Write them down. Read them out loud. Memorize them until you not only know them by heart, but you feel as if you are living them. When you do, you will always be close to something wonderful.

Never Too Much

The wonder of a changed perspective

*W*hen we hurt, we want things to change right away. But this is often when we hear things like "Have faith!" Under troubling circumstances, the translation of this is "Be patient." When there is a desperate need for connection with our Creator, the last thing we want to do is wait. "I demand an answer now!" is what we're really thinking, even though our words may sound humble and calm. Although we've all been told that prayers are answered in God's time not ours, we still wish for an instant, immediate response that is both memorable and visible. When that happens, our perspective is changed forever. And that's wonderful.

"I TEND TO BE THE STRONG ONE in my family, since I have training in crisis counseling," Penny says. "I've served as the mental health specialist for a critical incident team, where I've debriefed law enforcement officers, firefighters, and EMTs. Since I have so many specialized skills in this area, I thought I'd be able to work through most personal crises. But it wasn't that easy."

A few years ago in May, Penny's talents and patience were tested to the limit. First, her entire family, including children, parents, siblings, aunts, uncles, cousins, and in-laws, had their lives upended by a major flood. "My sons lost everything they owned. My parents' home was severely damaged, and we watched my aunt's house float down the river," Penny says. Through it all, Penny served as her family's anchor. "I was the strength for everyone who needed me."

Six weeks later, her parents' home was repaired. But tragically, her mother was killed in a car accident one day after the house was completed. Within a few more months, Penny's beloved grandfather died. Then her cousin's wife died during labor. Penny was devastated, but managed to carry on in spite of her many losses.

Then the "ultimate" tragedy occurred. "My twin grandsons, Tyler and Gunner, died at birth. I could not console my daughter or myself. I questioned my professional crisis intervention skills. Personally and emotionally, I felt totally overwhelmed."

Penny continued to visit her father and daughter weekly at their homes along what she began to call "the road of tears." She used the long drive to reflect on all that had recently happened to her and her family, but as she did, the pain simply grew greater. "One day I drove home overwhelmed in anguish," she says. "I cried the entire trip. As I drove, I yelled and screamed at God for all of the pain and loss my family and I had experienced. As I neared home, I reached a point where I could no longer bear the pain. My heart just couldn't take any more. I slammed my fists on the steering wheel and cried out to heaven, 'This is too much! This is more than I can bear! This is much too much!'"

That's when something wonderful happened.

"At the precise moment I cried, 'This is much too much,' a car similar to my son's car pulled up beside me. I thought for a moment it was him and wondered why he was out when he was supposed to be home, several miles away. The car passed me, pulling in quite close so I could see it clearly. At the exact moment I had cried, 'This is much too much!' the car pulled ahead, and I could see its license plate. It said "NVR2MH" (Never Too Much). I could not believe my eyes."

Penny pulled over to the side of the road and wrote down the license plate letters several times. "I still could not believe what I had just seen," she admits. "I dialed my cell phone to call a friend in law enforcement to tell her what had just happened and asked if she would please run the plate. She refused to do that, as she said she didn't want to mess with divine intervention."

Penny's grief was more manageable after that. "I will never forget how the response came in precise timing to my plea," she says. "And I will always remember that no matter what happens, it's never too much."

☯ *Love Light: Letting It Out*

Most of us are told that it is best to keep our grief under control. Unhappy children are often soothed with the words, "Don't cry. Please don't cry." We admire those who can lose someone they love and "be strong" or "keep it together," which both mean "don't cry." Although other cultures not only permit but encourage wailing and moaning in times of loss, unrestrained vocal or visible expressions of sorrow tend to make people uncomfortable in the United States.

It takes great energy to hold back what amounts to a tidal wave of emotion. The time and effort we spend trying to hide or control our sadness takes away from the wonders of love that could enter if only we hadn't erected a brick wall in front of them.

I have never met a person who has not suffered some kind of loss in his or her life. Sometimes it is the loss of one or more loved ones, but it can also be related to finances, a job, health, or love. Just like Penny, I know in my own life that, more than once, I have felt that my losses were too much. But I can honestly say that I have never pounded on a steering wheel or cried out to God. Instead, I took all my raw, angry energy, and exploded it in journals or on blank computer pages that I later erased.

If you want something wonderful to happen, let out your grief. Do so not to receive a sign from God, but because you deliver yourself to life when you stop trying to hide your true self from it. If you feel uncomfortable expressing yourself fully in front of other people, go in a room and close the door before you start ranting and raving. Take a shower and let your tears flow with the pounding water. Drive out to a rural area and give a good yell. Pound out your anger in a journal, then burn it so the ashes may carry away your hurt. Hold nothing back. You will know when enough is enough.

When your perspective has shifted, return to life. For as it says in Ecclesiastes: "There is a time for every purpose under heaven." And that's wonderful.

Love Arrives

The wonder of letting down your defenses

By now, I hope a twinkling belief has been born in your heart that wonder is closer than you may have thought. Love is all around, here to serve us whenever we are ready. So I will close this book with a story that sums up the three ways I know that bring wonder and its lessons of love into your life: by changing your perspective, acknowledging the wishes of your heart, and doing the thing you think you cannot do. Embrace any one of these, and watch as your life becomes more wonderful. Do all three, and "miracles" might come your way.

MARIA HAD GIVEN UP on the thought of ever being married. She had a child out of wedlock at age twenty. The baby's father had no interest in helping Maria parent her daughter, and she never heard from him again. She decided she was meant to devote herself to raising the baby alone and pursue a career in singing. "I put my own wants on the back burner and went forward serving others," she says.

Maria put on weight after the baby was born, but it didn't slow her busy life. She studied with legendary voice teachers and eventually earned her way onto the stage of the Metropolitan Opera in New York. But the singing business was harsh, and Maria soon got tired of the constant judgments and criticism that were being leveled at her not only for her singing, but also her weight. So she left New York for Indiana, where she joined the faculty of a major university while she pursued a Master's degree in vocal performance.

By the time she was in high school, Maria's daughter, Maura, wanted to be closer to Maria's large family in North Dakota. Maria agreed to move, and the two returned to Maria's hometown, where Maria took the risk of starting a singing school to support them.

Maria's Bel Canto Studio was a huge success, attracting hundreds of students and a long waiting list of others who wanted to study with her. Maria worked seven days a week, accommodating everyone's schedule as best she could as she tried to provide for her daughter. "Everyone came before I did," she admits.

Maria dated a little as her daughter grew up, but she never did so seriously. "I always wanted a soul connection with someone," she says, "but I was self-conscious about my weight."

To let off some internal steam after her busy days and nights, Maria enjoyed surfing the Internet. One of her favorite chat rooms was where people insulted each other. "It was all good fun. Everyone's anonymous, so it's really a game of how clever you can be." Maria liked to listen to the banter, especially since her computer was capable of broadcasting the dialogue. Then one night, as she was listening, something wonderful happened.

"There was a man with a Scottish brogue who was incredibly interesting," she says. "I was drawn both to his wit and his accent, so I I.M.'d him (sent an instant message), and we began to chat alone."

Colin found he was equally attracted to Maria. "I liked the witty way she talked and her intelligence," he says, "and just the way she carried herself." As the nights and the instant messages increased, Maria and Colin found they had a lot of mutual likes and dislikes, and a strong friendship developed.

Within a month, Colin started calling Maria, and the two would often talk four or five hours a night. "The phone bills were horrendous," Maria says, "but it was worth it. He was funny and intelligent, and I had a real comfortable feeling every time we talked."

Colin agrees. "I'm basically a shy person, and Maria helped me see my potential. 'You don't know what you've got within yourself,' she said. I was working for a man I despised and was getting severely depressed about my job. Because of her, I found the courage to quit."

Eventually, Maria stopped dating others, and Colin broke up with the woman he had been seeing. Soon, the pair started cautiously hinting about marriage. "We took it very, very slowly," Maria says. "I had been hurt before, and so had he. Besides, we weren't children. We were both in our thirties, and I had a teenage child. On top of that, we were from two different countries. There were geographical, cultural, religious, and family issues that had to be considered."

Maria and Colin took their relationship forward one day at a time. "I had a hard time saying 'I love you,' " Colin admits. "It became something of a joke between Maria and me. So when she would say it, I would just say 'thank you,' and we'd both laugh. I had pain from past relationships, and she helped me look more within myself and deal with my self-doubt and self-loathing."

The same was true for Maria. "Colin is tenacious, and so if I tried to close off or make excuses, he wouldn't let me. Originally, I had more vision about our relationship than he, but eventually he was the one with the strength who pulled me through moments of doubt."

As months passed, both Maria and Colin could see positive changes that came from their relationship. "I'm definitely more upbeat now than I was before I met Maria," Colin says. "Even my parents have seen a change in me." He once had trouble sleeping, but as the relationship progressed, his sleeping problems disappeared.

Maria made some bold moves, buying the house of her dreams and a sporty new car. "I realized that I didn't need permission from others to be happy and have the things I wanted," she says.

As the two worked out major issues, the idea of marriage seemed more likely. They started discussing a date when either Maria could fly to Scotland or Colin could come to America. Colin made the bold move of deciding to try a new life. He put his house up for sale, sold his possessions, and bought a plane ticket.

"That made it real," Maria says. "I knew exactly what date he was coming."

Once the couple decided to let love lead the way, the wonders flowed abundantly. Maria called the local university to inquire about Colin taking classes and was amazed by the Scottish brogue of the woman who answered the phone. "Colin and I had been concerned that he might be homesick, but here was a person who said she knew plenty of other Scottish people in the area."

Colin was worried about money. Not only did he not want to have Maria support him, but he hoped to be able to fly his parents to the U.S. for the wedding. Again wonder led the way. "I suddenly started finding out about all sorts of money I didn't know I had," he said, "like a government pension and cash I would be able to take away from the sale of my house."

Even as the pieces of their life together fell into place, Maria had concerns. She and Colin had discussed her weight before, and he had seen her both on a videophone and in pictures, so he knew what his bride-to-be looked like. He made it clear to her that he loved *her*, not a particular weight or size, and that he had no expectations of her losing weight or changing for him. But then something wonderful happened in disguise. When Maria's mother voiced concerns that her daughter might be hurt if Colin rejected her after meeting in person, Colin immediately called Maria's mother and made his intentions and feelings known.

Now, many lives have been transformed for the better. "It seemed for years like I was just treading water," Colin says. "But now the sum is greater than its parts."

"I'm amazed when I realize that you can assert your will and have the universe answer," Maria says.

"My paternal grandmother once told me, 'What is for you won't get by you,' " Colin says. "Dreams do come true."

Love Light: Letting Love Enter

I recently received an e-mail filled with a wonderful message. It was the story of a man who wanted to know God. "Let me hear You, God," he whispered, and a meadowlark began to sing. But the man didn't notice. Frustrated, he called out, "God! Speak to me!" and there was a clap of thunder. Again, the man did not listen. So he said, "God, let me see You," and a star twinkled in the sky. Once more, he did not notice. So he cried, "Show me a miracle, God!" and a baby was born. He paid no attention. So in desperation, he screamed, "Touch me, God, and let me know You are here!" And a butterfly landed on his shoulder. He brushed it away.

Wonders are everywhere, given to us by our Creator for our pleasure and peace. If you want more of them in your life, simply lift the veil of your resistance and you will see for yourself.

To do that, remember this simple fact: You cannot think two thoughts at the same time. It is biologically impossible. So if you are thinking about fear, you cannot be thinking about what makes you feel safe. If you are angry or upset with someone, you cannot be thinking about love. If you are thinking about how little money you have, you cannot be open for abundance to enter.

Whatever you think over and over becomes what you believe. If you want wonder to enter your life, you must believe it is possible. Ultimately, your beliefs are the only things that will prevent or attract wonders, for they not only color everything you think, say, and do, but they also create the vibrations that emanate from you to others.

Just for today, believe the best. Let love enter. Like Maria and Colin, you can get to know it slowly, surely. There's no rush—you have your whole life to enjoy it. Relax. Take a deep breath and let your soul have some air. Something wonderful is about to happen.

Believe it.

Has something wonderful ever happened to you?

I would love to hear your stories and share them in my next book. Feel free to write to me:

Robin L. Silverman
P.O. Box 13135
Grand Forks, ND 58208-3135